# HOW THE GOSPEL SPREAD
# THROUGH EUROPE

# HOW THE GOSPEL SPREAD THROUGH EUROPE

BY
## CHARLES H. ROBINSON, D.D.

HON. CANON OF RIPON AND EDITORIAL SECRETARY OF
THE SOCIETY FOR THE PROPAGATION OF THE
GOSPEL IN FOREIGN PARTS

WIPF & STOCK · Eugene, Oregon

Wipf and Stock Publishers
199 W 8th Ave, Suite 3
Eugene, OR 97401

How the Gospel Spread Through Europe
By Robinson, Charles H.
ISBN 13: 978-1-4982-2586-1
Publication date 4/6/2015
Previously published by SPCK, 1919

# NOTE

IN the present volume I have attempted to present, in a popular form, the story of the work accomplished by the missionaries to whom the evangelization of Europe was due. My object has been to emphasize the labours of typical missionaries together with the salient features of their work, and no attempt has been made to present a complete sketch of the spread of Christianity throughout Europe. I have also omitted all references to the original authorities on which the information provided in regard to each separate country is based. For these, and for a more complete account of the various subjects here discussed, I would venture to refer the reader to a larger volume recently published by Longmans, entitled "The Conversion of Europe." In cases in which the present volume is used by Study Circles the leader of the Circle will find in the larger volume information that may be needed to supplement that which is here given.

"Outlines for the Use of Study Circles" and "Suggestions to Leaders" based upon this volume have been issued.

C. H. R.

# CONTENTS

| CHAPTER | | PAGE |
|---|---|---|
| | NOTE | v |
| | LIST OF MAPS | 3 |
| I. | INTRODUCTORY | 5 |
| II. | THE BALKAN PENINSULA | 14 |
| III. | ITALY | 24 |
| IV. | SPAIN | 32 |
| V. | FRANCE | 40 |
| VI. | IRELAND | 53 |
| VII. | SCOTLAND | 59 |
| VIII. | ENGLAND | 66 |
| IX. | HOLLAND | 88 |
| X. | DENMARK | 93 |
| XI. | AUSTRIA | 98 |
| XII. | GERMANY | 109 |
| XIII. | SCANDINAVIA: | |
| | NORWAY | 137 |
| | SWEDEN | 142 |
| XIV. | RUSSIA | 146 |
| XV. | A GENERAL SURVEY | 159 |
| XVI. | RESULTS OF CHRISTIAN MISSIONS IN EUROPE | 167 |
| | INDEX | 177 |

*b*

# LIST OF MAPS

| | FACING PAGE |
|---|---|
| THE BALKAN PENINSULA IN THE FIFTH CENTURY | 5 |
| WESTERN EUROPE AT THE END OF THE SEVENTH CENTURY | 40 |
| ENGLAND IN THE SEVENTH CENTURY | 66 |
| CENTRAL EUROPE IN THE FOURTH CENTURY | 98 |
| CENTRAL EUROPE AT THE END OF THE NINTH CENTURY | 110 |
| THE BALTIC PROVINCES EARLY IN THE THIRTEENTH CENTURY | 142 |

To face page 5

# HOW THE GOSPEL SPREAD THROUGH EUROPE

## I

### INTRODUCTORY

TO many persons who are familiar with the missionary labours of St. Paul and of the other apostles, which are recorded in the New Testament, the story of what happened after their time and of the efforts that were made to carry on their work throughout Europe, is a complete blank. They have heard or read of St. Augustine's mission to England, and have some knowledge of what was accomplished by other missionaries in Great Britain, but of missionary work on the continent of Europe they know nothing. The loss that arises from this ignorance is great, for the story of the conversion of Europe, if it could be adequately told, would form the most wonderful and most inspiring book which, apart from the Bible, has ever been written.

**Deeds of heroism.**—If the story of the past could be completely unrolled it would be made manifest that no deeds of heroism, or endurance, or sacrifice for the good of others have been performed upon this earth which can outshine those that have been performed by the Christian missionaries to whom the evangelization of Europe was due.

Wherever the foot of man has trod the missionary has followed, inspired by love to his Master and by the belief that the revelation of His love is the one only cure for the world's sorrow. He has traversed seas, threaded his way through forests, braved starvation and want amidst hostile tribes; misunderstood, ridiculed, persecuted, and tortured, he has shown himself to be the sympathetic friend of all and has ministered to the wants alike of their souls and their bodies. He has shunned no difficulty and been daunted by no danger, but has rebuked sin, worked righteousness and wrought reform amongst all races with whom he has lived. His only visible weapon of attack has been a book, his only means of defence the shield of prayer. Whilst conscious of his many shortcomings and repeated failures, he has been upheld by the conviction that amidst all his sorrows and difficulties his divine Master walked ever by his side, and by the knowledge that the task to which He called him was divine.

It is true that the accounts relating to the work of the early missionaries that have been preserved are sadly deficient, and that of those which exist many were written so long after the events which they describe that they cannot be regarded as history; but, even so, enough remains to enable us to understand the nature of the task which they accomplished and to make us feel that there is no name of which any human being may be more humbly proud than that of Christian missionary.

**Missions in the first century.**—We gather from the New Testament that at the time of St. Paul's death, *i.e.* about 68 A.D., the gospel had been preached, and a Christian community had come into existence, in half a dozen towns in Macedonia and Greece, in three or four towns in Italy, and possibly in one or two places in Gaul (France), and Spain. In Asia Minor Churches had been established in a number of towns on or near its western and north-western coasts, and in Phrygia and Lycaonia in the south-east, also in the north, unless, as is probable, Galatia is to be identified with these provinces. There were also a certain number of Churches in Syria and Palestine. It can be shown that by the year 100 there were Christian communities in at least twelve places in Syria and Palestine, twenty-one in Asia Minor, and nine in the Balkan Peninsula.

*Apostolic Missionaries.*—Of the missionary work done by the apostles, beyond what is described in the New Testament, we know hardly anything.

There is no good reason to doubt that *St. Paul* fulfilled his intention of preaching the gospel in Spain (Rom. xv. 24-28, 2 Cor. I. 17). St. Clement of Rome, writing about thirty years after his death, says that St. Paul reached the farthest bounds of the west, an expression which at the time when he wrote was generally applied to Spain. The existence of a party in Corinth which said of him, "I am of Peter," suggests that *St. Peter* had worked as a missionary in Greece. Moreover, Dionysius, who was Bishop of Corinth in 170, speaks of the plantation of Peter and Paul at Rome and Corinth. We may also accept as probable the tradition that St. Peter visited Rome and died there.

Another tradition, which is also probably correct, states that *St. Thomas* preached the gospel in the district ruled by a Parthian chief named Gondophares, which lay between Persia and the river Indus. In later time his name was confused with that of a bishop called Thomas, who came from Edessa in 345, and landed on the coast of Malabar, together with a band of missionaries; and the apostle was eventually credited with having founded a church in South India.

A tradition, which apparently originated in the seventh century, states that *St. James* (who was put to death by Herod) preached the gospel in Spain, and he is to-day regarded as the Patron Saint of that country. An equally unhistorical tradition asserts that *St. Andrew* introduced Christianity into Russia. Eusebius, who wrote in the fourth century, states that the Evangelist *St. Mark* preached the gospel in Alexandria, and this statement may perhaps be true.

There are numerous traditions relating to the missionary activities of others whose names are mentioned in the New Testament, *e.g.* Lazarus and Joseph of Arimathea, but these are of such late origin and in many cases so improbable that it is not worth while to mention them.

**Unofficial missionaries.**—The greater part of the missionary work that was done during the two or three centuries which followed the times of the apostles was done by men and women who would not to-day be called missionaries, and who were engaged in the ordinary occupations of life. The lives and deaths of such Christians were in fact the chief means of spreading the Christian faith. Tertullian's statement that "the blood of Christians is seed" was proved true again and again, nor can it be denied that the more any given Church was persecuted the greater became its efficiency from a missionary standpoint; but if the martyrdoms of Christians provided occasional impulses towards the expansion of the Christian Church, the loving sympathy which they displayed towards each other and the high moral standard of their lives exerted an even greater influence. Justin Martyr tells us that it was as a result of witnessing the moral lives and fearless deaths of the Christians that he himself became a Christian, and his experience was shared by many others.

We may, perhaps, interpret the allusion in the third Epistle of St. John to those who, "for the sake of the Name, went forth taking nothing of the Gentiles," as referring to missionaries who were accustomed to receive nothing from those whom they sought to convert. The writings of the early fathers contain hardly more than a few fragmentary references to the missionary activities of the early Christians. Eusebius, referring to the missionary work carried on by the generation of Christians which succeeded that of the apostolic age, writes: "Very many of the disciples of that age (pupils of the apostles) whose heart had been ravished by the divine Word with a burning love for philosophy (*i.e.* asceticism) had first fulfilled the command of the Saviour and divided their goods among the needy. Then they set out on long journeys performing the office of evangelists, eagerly striving to preach Christ to those who, as yet, had never heard the word of faith, and to deliver to them the holy gospels. In foreign lands they merely laid the foundations of the faith, and afterwards appointed others as shepherds, entrusting them with the care of those who had been recently brought into (the Church), while they themselves proceeded with the grace and co-operation of God to other countries, and to other peoples."

In some instances Christianity was first commended to pagans by their slaves, or by those whom they had captured in war. The Church historian Sozomen, writing about 440, refers thus to the influence exerted by the lives of Christians which resulted in the spread of Christianity in the Balkan Peninsula, and his description would apply to many other parts of Europe.

"To almost all the barbarians the opportunity of having Christian teaching proclaimed to them was offered by the war which took place at that time between the Romans and the other races, under the reign of Gallienus and his successors. For when in those reigns an untold multitude of mixed races passed over from Thrace, and overran Asia, while from different quarters different barbarian peoples treated in like manner the Romans who were their neighbours, many priests of Christ were taken prisoners and abode with them. And when they healed the sick who were there, cleansed those who had evil spirits by simply naming the name of Christ and calling on the Son of God, and further maintained a noble and blameless conversation, and overcame their reproach by their virtuous conduct, the barbarians marvelled at the men, their life and wonderful works and acknowledged that they themselves would be wise and win the favour of God if they were to act after the manner of those who thus showed themselves to be better men, and like them were to serve the right : so, getting them to instruct them in their duty, they were taught and baptized and subsequently met as a congregation."

**Monks as missionaries.**—The first men of whom we know any particulars and who can be described as regular missionaries were monks. Monasticism, which was first developed in Egypt, was introduced into Italy by Athanasius and his followers, in the middle of the fourth century, and a few years later the first monastery in Gaul was founded by St. Martin of Tours near Poitiers ; and by the end of the fifth century monasteries had been established in nearly all the provinces of the Roman Empire. During the fifth century there occurred a great decline in the spiritual life and influence of the monasteries, but a revival took place subsequently which was largely due to the influence of Benedict and his followers.

It is hard to conceive how, under the conditions that prevailed in Europe in early and mediæval times, the missionary work accomplished by the monks could have been accomplished by any other agency. If, on the one hand, their inability to set before the pagans the picture of a Christian home tended to produce a one-sided type of Christianity, on the other hand, the life which they led as Christian communities exerted a continuous and far-reaching influence. Thus Dr. Skene, comparing the evangelistic methods adopted by individual missionaries and by those who lived together as monks, writes : " The monastic missionaries did not commence their work, as the earlier secular Church would have done, by arguing against their idolatry, superstition, and immorality, and preaching a purer faith, but they opposed to it the antagonistic characteristics and purer life of Christianity. They exhibited a life of purity, holiness, and self-denial. They exercised charity and benevolence, and they forced the respect of the surrounding pagans to a life, the motives of which they could not comprehend, unless they resulted from principles higher than those their pagan religion afforded them ; and, having won their respect for their lives and their gratitude for their benevolence, these monastic missionaries went among them with the Word of God in their hands, and preached to them the doctrines and pure morality of the Word of Life."

**The use of physical force.**—In studying the history of the conversion of Europe we cannot fail to be impressed by the large part which the employment of physical force played in the spread of Christianity. Before the year 312 physical force was frequently employed by the pagans in order to prevent the growth of the Christian Church, but within fifty years of this time Christians were found who advocated the employment of force in order to compel pagans to accept the Christian faith. Although from time to time a few voices were raised against attempts to convert people by force, it gradually came to be accepted by the rulers of the Christian Church that where persuasion failed force might be employed, and its use became more and more common.

Great Britain and Ireland are the only countries in Europe in which the profession of Christianity was not at one time or another spread by the threat of persecution and death. Ireland appears to be the only country which has witnessed no Christian martyrdom. The worst instances of the use of compulsion are to be found in Prussia, Pomerania, and Scandinavia. In Norway King Hakon hastened the nominal acceptance of Christianity by burning to death those who refused to be converted, whilst in Prussia the "Christian" Knights of the Sword ravaged the country for decades of years with a view to the conversion of its inhabitants.

In other cases, as, for example, in Russia, although no actual violence was used, thousands of persons were baptized at one time, in obedience to an order issued by their ruler, who had received little instruction, and whose lives were in no way affected by the change in their religious profession. In view of the haste with which whole communities, or tribes, were sometimes enrolled as Christians there is no cause for surprise that pagan reactions constantly occurred.

**Influence of Constantine.**—The battle of the Milvian Bridge (October 28, 312), as a result of which Constantine became the ruler of the Roman Empire, marks an epoch in the development of Christianity in Europe. From this time forward the Christian Church was left free to expand, but from this time forward it was deprived of the bracing and purifying influence which the contempt and the persecution of the State had before exerted upon its members. It has been said, and there is a measure of truth in the statement, that the conversion of Constantine was the greatest calamity that ever happened to the Church. Although he was a sagacious and powerful ruler, his standard of life and conduct was miserably low. Many years after his alleged conversion he murdered his own wife Fausta and his son Crispus, and he committed numerous other crimes of which those who made no profession of Christianity would have been ashamed. His conversion resulted in the rapid extension of a profession of Christianity throughout the Empire; but, as might have been expected, the conversion of his subjects was no deeper or more complete than was his own. As far as we can judge when we look back upon the past, it would have been better for the religious interests of Europe as a whole if Constantine had not professed the Christian faith, and if the Christians had continued for another century or more to be a persecuted and despised sect. John Stewart Mill, wrote, " It is one of the most tragical facts of all history that Constantine, rather than Marcus Aurelius, was the first Christian Emperor." Had the influence which induced many to call themselves Christian been purer, and had the missionaries and early Christian teachers succeeded in inspiring their converts with the true ideals of Christianity, the subsequent history of Europe would have been far other than it has been.

**Conversion of the Upper Classes.**—With very few exceptions the conversion of Europe was brought about by missionary influences that spread from the upper and better educated to the lower and less educated classes. The principle enunciated by one of the Pomeranian dukes during a missionary tour made by Bishop Otto in his country was generally recognized and acted upon. The duke said: " It is for us who are the chiefs and men of importance to have regard to our dignity and to agree together in regard to this most deserving matter, so that the people who are subject to us may be instructed by our example. For whatever religion or virtue is to be attempted I say that it is more correct that it should pass from the head to the members than from the members to the head. In the primitive Church, indeed, as we have heard, the Christian faith began with the common people and with individuals belonging to the common people, and spread to the middle classes, and then affected the chiefs of the world. Let us reverse the custom of the primitive Church so that the holiness of the divine religion, beginning with us who are chiefs and passing on to the middle classes by an easy progress, may enlighten the whole people and race."

The reasoning of the Pomeranian duke was plausible, but the experience of missionaries in ancient and modern times has been that when a religion has been accepted by a people because it has been recommended to them by their rulers, it is most likely to become superficial and to fail to affect their characters.

The earliest Christian communities in Europe were first established in the countries that border upon the Mediterranean. We shall therefore begin our account of the spread of Christianity throughout Europe with these countries.

## II

## THE BALKAN PENINSULA

EARLY Christian communities.—Before the end of the first century, Christian communities had been established at Philippi, Thessalonica, and Beroea in Macedonia ; Nicopolis in Epirus ; Athens, Corinth, and Cenchrea in Greece ; and in Illyria and Dalmatia. All these places are mentioned in the New Testament. Two centuries later the number of bishoprics in Greece was at least twenty, but of the missionary activities by which the Christian faith had been spread we know nothing.

Polycarp, bishop of Smyrna, addressed a letter to the Christians at Philippi just before his martyrdom in 155, in which he exhorted them to beware of covetousness and reminded them of the teaching which had been given them by St. Paul. Origen, who visited Athens in 230, wrote, " The Church of God at Athens is a peaceable and orderly body, as it desires to please Almighty God." On the other hand, Gregory of Nazianzus, who was educated at Athens in the middle of the fourth century, refers to the strength of paganism and pagan teaching at that time. The Church which St. Paul founded at Corinth continued to expand after his death. Thus Clement, bishop of Rome, writing to the Church at Corinth in 95, after referring to the " detestable and unholy sedition " that had arisen in their midst, praises them for their " steadfast faith," and that they were " ready unto every good work." Hegesippus, a Jewish Christian, writing about 180, says that the Church of the

Corinthians continued in the orthodox faith. Christianity spread slowly throughout the country districts, the last people to be converted being the Slavonic tribe to whom missionaries were sent by the Emperor Basil about 870. Long before this the Emperor Justinian had issued orders that all who had not been baptized were to assemble in churches together with their wives and children, and, after receiving instruction, were to be baptized forthwith. Those who refused to be baptized were to be deprived of all their property, and, if convicted of sacrificing to idols, were to be put to death.

Although Constantinople was founded by a Christian Emperor, and had no heathen traditions, many heathen were discovered to be living there as late as 561, when all who were discovered were forcibly baptized.

**Ulfilas.**—We come now to consider the work accomplished by one of the greatest of the missionaries to whom the conversion of Europe was due, Ulfilas, the Apostle of the Goths. The Goths, starting from the southern shores of the Baltic Sea, invaded Moesia, which included the northern parts of Serbia and Bulgaria, about the year 250. They also settled in the Crimea, where a few of them became Christians. Ulfilas, who was born about 311 and was brought up amongst the Goths, was sent by them, in 332, either as an envoy or as a hostage, to Constantinople, where he learnt Latin and Greek. After working as a missionary amongst his own countrymen in Constantinople and its neighbourhood he was consecrated as a bishop in 341, and for the next seven years he served as a missionary in Dacia, which includes modern Roumania, but in 348 so bitter a persecution was raised against the Christians that Ulfilas sought and obtained permission for the Christian Goths to cross the Danube and settle within the borders of the Roman Empire, that is in Bulgaria. Of the work done by Ulfilas amongst the Goths who crossed the Danube, we have unfortunately no information. His work amongst the Goths north of the Danube was interrupted by his enforced flight, but by his homilies and treatises, and, later on, by his Bible translations and through the work of his disciples, he continued to exert a considerable influence, and it was doubtless due to his efforts and inspiration that their number continued steadily to increase. The Christians who were in touch with Ulfilas were regarded as Arians, but missionary work was also carried on by representatives of the Orthodox party, and in the persecution raised by Athanaric, king of the Goths, at the end of 369, and which continued for four years, many suffered death who were followers of Athanasius.

Of the Christians who suffered during this persecution some were brought to trial and boldly confessed their faith, whilst others were killed without having been afforded an opportunity of witnessing for Christ. In one district a wooden idol was placed upon a cart, and was taken from village to village, and the Christians were summoned to come forth and worship and offer sacrifices to the idol. When they refused the heathen burnt the houses with the Christians inside. One of those who suffered, and who belonged apparently to the Orthodox party, was *St. Saba*, who had been a Christian from his boyhood. When the heathen arrived at his village, his friends, who desired to protect him from their fury, swore that there were no Christians in the village; but he suddenly appeared, and said openly, " Let no one swear for me, for I am a Christian." On this occasion he was allowed to go free on the ground that he was so poor and obscure that he could do neither good nor harm. Later on, however, he was carried off, together with a priest named Sansala, and having refused to eat meat that had been offered to idols he was eventually drowned in the river Musæus.

**A Gothic Bible.**—The work by means of which Ulfilas exerted the widest and most enduring influence, and which distinguished him from all his missionary predecessors, was his translation of the Bible into the Gothic language. The importance and significance of this work of translation has been well described by Professor Max Muller, who wrote: "Ulfilas must have been a man of extraordinary power to conceive, for the first time, the idea of translating the Bible into the vulgar language of his people. At this time there existed in Europe but two languages which a Christian bishop would have thought himself justified in employing, Greek and Latin. All other languages were still considered as barbarous. It requires a prophetic insight and a faith in the destinies of those half-savage tribes, and a conviction also of the utter effeteness of the Roman and Byzantine Empires, before a bishop could have brought himself to translate the Bible into the vulgar dialect of his barbarous countrymen." Translations of the Bible or of parts of the Bible had previously been made into Syrian and Egyptian dialects, but these were already literary languages. Ulfilas was the first to translate the Bible into a language in which no literature of any kind existed at the time. He not only translated the Bible into Gothic, but is said to have invented the characters in which the translation was written.

It is interesting to note that when translating the Old Testament he omitted the books of the Kings and Chronicles for fear lest the warlike tendencies of his converts should be encouraged by reading of wars that had received divine sanction.

**The work of Ulfilas.**—Auxentius, the biographer of Ulfilas, tells us almost nothing concerning his methods of work, but he sums up his all too brief account thus: "Preaching and giving thanks with love to God the Father through Christ he flourished gloriously for forty years in his bishopric, and with apostolic grace he preached in the Greek and Latin and Gothic languages without intermission in the one only Church of Christ, for one is the Church of the living God, the pillar and ground of the truth, and he used to assert and contend that one is the flock of Christ our Lord and God, one husbandry, one building, one virgin, one spouse, one kingdom, one vineyard, one house, one temple, one assembly of Christians, all other meetings being not churches of God but synagogues of Satan."

In 381, when he was now seventy years of age, Ulfilas was summoned by the Emperor Theodosius to attend a council at Constantinople. A dispute had arisen amongst the Arians in Constantinople, and it was hoped that Ulfilas, who was a semi-Arian, might be able to mediate. His long-continued labours had already weakened his health, and on reaching Constantinople he died before he had attempted to fulfil the object for which he had been summoned. His biographer writes: "It behoves us to consider the merit of the man who by the guidance of the Lord came to die at Constantinople, nay, rather at Christianople, so that the holy and stainless priest of Christ might, conformably to his merits, be marvellously and splendidly honoured by saints and fellow-priests, the worthy man in worthy fashion by worthy men, and at the hands of so great a multitude of Christians."

The figure of Ulfilas, in so far as we can discern it through the mists of time, and as it is portrayed in the writings of his prejudiced opponents, is that of a man who rose far above the atmosphere of religious controversy which distinguished his age, and who devoted his life to active toil, and his great literary powers to the provision of a version of the Sacred Scriptures which, whilst it has outlasted the political existence of his race, has provided an example and furnished a standard for all succeeding generations. Without undervaluing the work of his contemporary St. Martin of Tours, we may say that he was the greatest missionary who had laboured in Europe subsequent to the death of St. Paul. Selenas, who had been an assistant of Ulfilas, succeeded him as bishop, and for the next fifteen years the Goths lived a peaceful and settled life, whilst the followers and pupils of Ulfilas carried on his work, the fruits of which were seen in the subsequent development of the national character to which later historians were to bear warm testimony.

**Campaigns of the Goths.**—On the death of the Emperor Theodosius in 395 the Goths ceased to own allegiance to the Empire, and chose Alaric as their king. The greater part of those settled in Moesia probably followed Alaric in some of his many campaigns, and of those who remained some were induced by the missionaries sent out by Chrysostom to join the catholic Church. The Goths who overran Italy, Spain, and other countries were accompanied by Christian bishops, one of whom, *Sigesarius*, after the capture of Rome, baptized the Emperor Attalus, whilst another, named *Maximin*, was present with the Gothic troops at Carthage in 427. When the Goths invaded Gaul they established an extensive and well-organized Church to which Gregory of Tours frequently refers : they were keen, moreover, to act as missionaries amongst the pagans.

With the reception into the catholic Church of Reccared, the king of the Goths in Spain (586), the last branch of the Gothic Church came to an end, and the influence of the Goths as a factor in European history ceased to exist.

**Missionaries in Bulgaria**—After the death of Ulfilas in 381, no further attempt appears to have been made to convert the inhabitants of Bulgaria, and after a time the Christian Church there seems to have become extinct. Nearly 500 years elapsed before the arrival of the next Christian missionaries, and by this time the nationality of the population had greatly changed. Before the close of the seventh century the Bulgarians, who had originally come from central Asia, had occupied the greater part of Macedonia and Epirus. Having conquered the Slavonic inhabitants of these districts they adopted their language and customs and eventually, by intermarriage, became identified with them. Christianity was introduced amongst them in 813, when, in the course of a raid upon territory belonging to the Roman Empire, they captured Adrianople and carried captive a number of Christians, including a bishop. This bishop and many of his fellow-captives eventually died a martyr's death. After the lapse of nearly fifty years a monk named *Constantine Cypharas*, who had been carried captive by the Bulgarians, endeavoured to preach to them the Christian faith.

**Baptism of Bogoris.**—In 861 a sister of the Bulgarian Prince Bogoris (Boris), who had apparently been held as a captive at Constantinople for several years, and who had been baptized there as a Christian, was restored to her own country, Cypharas being at the same time released and sent back to Constantinople. She endeavoured, though at first without success, to impart to her brother her new faith, but eventually in a time of severe famine Bogoris was induced to solicit aid from the God of the Christians, and, the famine having come to an end, showed a disposition to listen to the entreaties of his sister that he should accept the Christian faith. According to a story, which is of doubtful historical value, the sister of Bogoris had sent for a skilful artist named *Methodius*, who has sometimes been identified with the well-known missionary to the Moravians, in order that he might paint some scenes to adorn the walls of Bogoris' palace. Cedrenus relates that Methodius, instead of painting hunting scenes on the walls of the palace as Bogoris had requested, produced a picture representing the final Judgment, the effect of which was so great that Bogoris expressed a desire to receive Christian instruction. He was baptized in 863 or 864 by the name Michael, the Emperor Michael (though not present on the occasion) being his godfather. His baptism took place at midnight, as it was feared that it might excite the forcible opposition of his subjects. After his baptism he received a long letter from Photius, the Patriarch of Constantinople, which was largely concerned with theological controversy, and in which he exhorted him to take measures for the conversion of his people. Contrary to the advice of Photius, who had urged him to abstain from recourse to force, he proceeded to compel them to follow his example, with the result that an insurrection occurred, which he suppressed with great cruelty, all the rebellious nobles and their families being massacred.

Photius had not apparently troubled to send any missionaries to assist Bogoris in the evangelization of the country, and several unauthorized and uneducated Greeks began to act as missionaries and teachers. One who pretended to be a priest baptized many, but when his followers discovered that he had deceived them they cut off his nose and ears and expelled him from their country. There arrived also Roman and Armenian missionaries who spoke against the teachings of the Greeks, and commended the doctrines of their own Churches. Moved, partly by the refusal of the Greek patriarch to consecrate a bishop for Bulgaria and partly by political reasons, Bogoris now applied for help (865) to Pope Nicholas I. and to the Emperor Louis II. of Germany. The Pope replied by sending two Italian bishops, Paul and Formosus, who took with them a detailed reply to a hundred and six questions that Bogoris had asked, relating to the conduct of converts to the Christian faith. The Pope's letter compares favourably with the letter which had been received from Photius, and displays an intelligent appreciation of the needs and difficulties of those who were striving to abandon heathen customs and to live a Christian life. Several of the questions asked by Bogoris and of the answers given by the Pope are of interest from a missionary standpoint, and throw light upon the conditions attaching to the work of the early missionaries both in Bulgaria and elsewhere.

**The Pope's Letter to Bogoris.**—The Pope rebukes

Bogoris for the cruelty with which he had suppressed the rebellion that had followed his own baptism, and specially for his massacre of women and children. He urges that those who were unwilling to abandon idolatry should be reasoned with and exhorted rather than coerced, inasmuch as " nothing can be good which is not the outcome of free action." God asks of man a voluntary obedience ; had He chosen to use force none could have resisted His will: intercourse with those who refused to become Christians must be avoided, and they must be left to God's judgment : but in the case of those who had become Christians and had fallen back into idolatry, force should be employed to reconvert them, as their case is similar to that of blasphemers who, according to the laws contained in the Old Testament, were to be punished with death.

The Pope defended the Greek whose nose and ears the Bulgarians had cut off on the ground that pious deception was lawful when the object in view was the conversion of heathen to the true faith.

It is possible that the Jesuit missionary, Robert di Nobili, who in the seventeenth century pretended to be a Brahman in India,* had in mind this official declaration of the Pope.

In reply to a question whether a number of baptisms which had been administered by a Jew, whose own conversion to Christianity was doubtful, were valid, the Pope urges their validity on the ground that they had been administered in the name of the Trinity.

In answer to the question asked him concerning the wearing of the cross, he explained that, as Christ had commanded that men should bear the cross in their hearts, they should also wear it on their bodies in order that they may be constantly reminded of their duty to bear it in their hearts. The wearing of the cross should denote

* See " History of Christian Missions," by the author, pp. 75 ff.

mortification of the flesh and compassion towards others.

The answer to one question, viz. that relating to the lawfulness of praying for the salvation of their forefathers, grates harshly upon our ears. It was similar to that given by Wulfram to the Frisian king Radbod. The Pope quotes the reference by St. John (1 John v. 16) to the "sin unto death," and says that such a mark of affection could not be allowed. In conclusion he promised to send them a bishop and later on perhaps a patriarch.

**Relations with the Greek Patriarch.**—After the return of the two bishops whom Pope Nicholas had sent, the Bulgarians still hesitated whether to ally themselves with Constantinople or with Rome. The patriarch Photius claimed their allegiance on the ground that he had baptized Bogoris, whilst the Pope claimed it on the ground that their country had always been within the limits of the Roman Empire. In a circular letter addressed to the patriarchs of Alexandria, Jerusalem, and Antioch, Photius denounced the intrusion of the Pope. In an earlier letter addressed to the bishops of the East in 869 he wrote: "Moreover the barbarous race of Bulgarians, which was hostile to Christ, is become so gentle and mindful of God that, abandoning their ancestral and devilish orgies and putting off the deceit of Hellenic superstition, contrary to all expectation they have been engrafted into the faith of Christians." At length, and notwithstanding the warnings of Pope John VIII., the Bulgarians finally threw in their lot with the Greek Church, and a Greek archbishop and Greek bishops were received and set over the Bulgarian Church.

During the reign of Simeon (893-927) the younger son of Bogoris, Christianity was established as the religion of Bulgaria.

# III

# ITALY

**INTRODUCTION of Christianity.**—Of the missionary activities which resulted in the conversion of Italy we know less than in the case of any other European country. Its conversion occupied six hundred years, but, outside the city of Rome, we do not know of any missionary who exerted a wide or lasting influence upon its peoples.

It is probable that a knowledge of the Christian faith was first introduced into Italy by some of the " sojourners of Rome," who listened to the preaching of St. Peter at Jerusalem on the day of Pentecost, and who would have carried back to Rome a report of what they had seen and heard. It was, perhaps, as a result of their influence that the Christian community came into existence to which St. Paul, writing about the year 57, sends greetings in the Epistle to the Romans.

That this community was inspired with missionary zeal may be inferred from his statement that its faith was " proclaimed throughout the whole world." Aristobulus and Narcissus, in whose houses Christians were to be found, were apparently Roman nobles, and, later on, when St. Paul himself was in Rome, there were Christians " in Cæsar's household." Tacitus, the Latin historian, referring to Nero's persecution of the Christians in 64, speaks of a great multitude of Christians, an expression which cannot have denoted less than several hundreds.

**St. Peter in Rome.**—There is no reason to doubt the early tradition that St. Peter visited and taught in Rome.

He may have become interested in the great city as the result of converse with those to whom he preached on the Day of Pentecost, or he may have obtained introductions to dwellers in Rome from Cornelius, the captain of the Italian Band, which consisted of volunteers from Italy. He may also have heard that Simon Magus, whom he had silenced in Samaria, was teaching and influencing many in Rome.

**Early Roman converts.**—Clement of Rome, writing to the Christians at Corinth about A.D. 95, after referring to the deaths of St. Peter and St. Paul, wrote: " Unto these men of holy lives was gathered a vast multitude of the elect, who, through many indignities and tortures, set a brave example among themselves." A Roman consul Titus Flavius Clemens and his wife Domitilla, who were closely related to the Emperor Domitian, were Christians and were punished as such (95-96).

There are many references, both in Christian and non-Christian writings, to prove that in the second, and still more in the third century, the number of Christians in Rome belonging to the richer and more cultured classes was considerable. Eusebius writes, " about the time of the reign of Commodus (180-192), our affairs changed for the better, and by God's grace the Churches all over the world enjoyed peace. Meanwhile the word of salvation was conducting every soul from every race of men to the devout worship of the God of all things, so that a large number of people at Rome, eminent for great wealth and high birth, turned to their salvation along with all their households and families." During the reign of Commodus a Christian named Carpophorus belonged to the Emperor's household, one of whose slaves, Callistus, afterwards became bishop of Rome.

**Early persecutions.**—A rescript issued by the Emperor Valerian in 258 suggests that there were many Christians belonging to the highest classes of Roman society. It reads: " Senators and prominent men and,

Roman knights are to lose their position and, moreover, be deprived of their property, and if they persist in being Christians after their goods have been taken away from them, they are to be beheaded. Matrons are to be deprived of their goods and sent into exile ; but members of Cæsar's household are to have their goods confiscated and be sent in chains by appointment to the estates of Cæsar."

The wife and daughter of the Emperor Diocletian, who became one of the chief persecutors (303-304), were Christians.

**Christian soldiers.**—Christianity in early times seemed specially to appeal to soldiers, and some of the most effective missionary work was done by them. Pachomius, who was one of the founders of monasticism, was a soldier in Constantine's army and was converted to Christianity by the brotherly love displayed by his fellow-soldiers. In the prayers of the early Church the Roman army was regularly mentioned, and, although there were always a few pacifists, the majority of the Christians did not regard the profession of a soldier as inconsistent with the practice of their religion.

One of the canons passed at the Council of Arles in Gaul (A.D. 314), pronounced sentence of excommunication upon any Christian soldier who should decline to perform his military duties.

**Greek-speaking Christians.**—In considering the spread of Christianity in Rome and Southern Italy we have to remember that for at least a hundred years after a Christian Church was established the majority of its members spoke Greek rather than Latin. When St. Paul was in Rome the upper classes spoke Greek in preference to Latin, and amongst the poorer classes a debased form of Greek was used for trade purposes. The first bishop of Rome who wrote in Latin was Victor (189-199), and of the bishops who preceded him only two bear Latin names. When Polycarp bishop of Smyrna reached Rome in 154 he conducted service there in Greek, and the Apostles' Creed was apparently composed in Greek about the middle of the second century. The majority of the Roman clergy appear to have used Greek as their official language till the middle of the third century. How soon the Bible was translated into Latin for the benefit of the Roman Christians it is impossible to discover, but it is probable that the Latin versions made in North Africa in the second century were earlier than any of the Italian versions.

**The number of Christians in Rome.**—We may obtain some idea as to the number of Christians to be found in Rome in 251 from a letter written by Cornelius, bishop of Rome, in which he states that there were then "forty-six presbyters, seven deacons, five sub-deacons, forty-two acolytes, fifty-two exorcists, readers, and door-keepers, and 1500 widows and persons in distress, all of whom the Master's grace and loving-kindness support."

It has been suggested that these figures point to a Christian community numbering about 30,000. In addition to these there were a certain number of Montanists and other Christians who were regarded by the orthodox Christians as heretics. The total number of bishops in Italy at this period was about one hundred. By the beginning of the fourth century almost every town of any considerable size in Italy had a Christian community, but of the missionary agents by whom the faith was spread we know nothing. Gaudentius, who was bishop of Brescia in 387, wrote, "It is clear that the heathen hastened with the celerity of a running wheel to leave the error of idolatry into which they had formerly sunk and to adopt Christian truth."

**The Catacombs.**—The number of Christians who were buried in the catacombs, the underground excavations outside Rome, affords some indication of the extent of the Christian population. The total length of the galleries has been reckoned at from 500 to 700 miles, and the number of burials at from one and a half to six millions.

There are no inscriptions later than 410, and by far the larger part of the tombs belongs to the century and a half which preceded the edict of Constantine in 313.

**Christianity in North Italy.**—That Christianity had spread throughout north Italy by the end of the fourth century is shown by the fact that in 396 Ambrose Bishop of Milan could write to the Church in Vercelli, " The Church of the Lord in your midst has not yet a priest, it being the only one that is deprived of the service of a priest in all Liguria, or Aemilia, or Venetia, or the other districts that border on Italy."

**Paganism in Rome.**—In 341 the first edict ordering heathen sacrifices to cease was issued by the Emperor Constantius, but as late as 395 temples to at least nine different heathen deities were standing in Rome, and festivals and ceremonies in connection with them were still observed.

Jerome, however, could write in 403, " The golden capitol is dishonoured, all the temples of Rome stand begrimed with cobwebs . . . and the populace streams past the half-demolished shrines on their way to the tombs of the martyrs."

**Suppression of pagan customs.**—In 408 the Emperor Honorius directed that all images in temples should be removed, the temples should be converted to secular uses, and the endowments of heathen festivals should be devoted to provide payment for the army. It is interesting to note that Augustine disapproved of the destruction of the temples which was ordered by this edict. He wrote, " Let us first extirpate the idolatry of the hearts of the heathen and they will either themselves assist us, or anticipate us in the execution of this good work. The bishops of the towns were empowered to suppress pagan customs, and the civil authorities were ordered to assist them. The edict was not, however, extensively enforced, and the next emperor of Rome, Attalus, was himself a pagan.

# ITALY

A belief in magic, divination, and astrology exercised a widespread influence in the later days of paganism, and long after paganism had been legally suppressed. The capture of Rome by the Goths under Alaric in 410 meant the final defeat of paganism in the city of Rome, though it lingered on for centuries in some of the country districts. As paganism died out throughout Italy many temples were converted into churches, and local deities were in some cases transformed into Christian saints. Moreover the reverence offered to the relics of martyrs and saints which gradually developed, was in many instances a continuation of worship that had before been offered to some pagan god.

**Attempts to revivify paganism.**—From the point of view of the modern Christian missionary the overthrow of paganism and the triumph of Christianity in Italy have a special interest, inasmuch as the final struggle that occurred between Christianity and paganism resembles in one important respect the struggle which is taking place to-day between Christianity and the religions of India and the Far East. The representatives of Hinduism, Buddhism, and Confucianism, realizing that Christian missionaries are making steady and increasing progress, and conscious that the moral teaching of Christianity is purer and nobler than that of any other religion, have tried to revise the teachings of their ancient faiths and to reinterpret all that is coarse and degrading in their sacred books in accordance with Christian standards.

They have thus produced rules of life and conduct worthy to be compared with those accepted by Christians, and have then endeavoured to show to those who might be disposed to accept the Christian faith that there was nothing distinctive in its teaching, which separated it from other religions, and that it could therefore make no claim upon their allegiance. As it is to-day in India and the Far East so it was in Italy and Greece during the fourth century. Men like the Emperor Julian, or the philosopher Libanius, sought to oppose a purified heathenism to the advancing tide of Christianity. Professor Lindsay writes : " Paganism never showed itself to greater advantage than during its last years of heroic but unavailing struggle. Its leaders, whether in the schools of Athens, or among the senatorial party at Rome, were for the most part men of pure lives with a high moral standard of conduct, men who commanded esteem and respect. Immorality abounded, but the pagan standard had become much higher. Christians and heathen were full of mutual esteem for each other." The efforts that are being made to stem the tide of Christian Missions in India are likely to share the same fate as those that were made long ago and for the same reason. The purified paganism of the fourth and fifth centuries and the rejuvenated Hinduism, Buddhism, or Confucianism of to-day had and have no gospel of hope for the poor, the degraded, and the miserable. The possession of this hope and of the power to impart it to others gave, and still gives, to Christianity its irresistible success as a missionary religion.

The Christian communities contained many unworthy members, and its best representatives were far from attaining to the standards of life which they accepted as incumbent upon them, but, despite all their failings, these communities were and are the embodiment of the only force which can regenerate human society.

**Paganism in Southern Italy.**—For a long time after the public worship of the heathen gods had ceased in Rome it continued in the country districts, and especially in Southern Italy. Naples was distinguished for its persistent adherence to paganism, and Etruria continued for a long time to supply the whole of Italy with pagan diviners. The abolition of the public worship of the gods in Southern Italy dates from about 500.

When Benedict arrived at the site of Monte Cassino in 529, prior to the foundation of the monastery, he found paganism still surviving. St. Gregory in his life of Benedict says that there existed there a very ancient shrine of Apollo, and a sacred wood where the foolish peasants worshipped Apollo and other demons. As the result of Benedict's preaching they cut down the sacred wood and destroyed the shrine and idol.

**Columbanus in Italy.**—So far as can be gathered from the records that have survived, Italy produced no great missionary who laboured for the conversion of its people. It can, however, claim to have furnished a home and a last resting-place to a great Irish missionary, Columbanus, the greater part of whose work was accomplished in the north-east of France. On leaving this district he worked for a while near Lake Constance, and in 613, accompanied by a single disciple named Attalus, he crossed the Alps and betook himself to the court of the Lombard king, Agiluf, at Milan.

In a secluded gorge of the Apennines between Genoa and Milan he founded, and helped with his own hands to build, the monastery of Bobbio which afterwards became widely famous. During his last days he laboured to win the Arians of Lombardy to the orthodox faith, and to convert the pagans who were still to be found in the neighbourhood. He eventually died at Bobbio in A.D. 615, at the age of 72.

[For further references to the life and work of Columbanus, see pp. 47–52.]

A cave is pointed out in a mountain gorge near Bobbio in which Columbanus is said to have lived towards the end of his life, only returning to the monastery to spend Sundays and Saints' Days with his brethren.

## IV

## SPAIN

**SPAIN'S Patron Saint.**—In the case of Spain we know hardly more concerning the beginning of missionary work than we know in the case of Italy.

Nearly all Spaniards believe that their country was first evangelized by the Apostle *James* (Iago), who was put to death by Herod, but the tradition is an impossible one, and was first suggested six hundred years after the death of St. James.

**St. Paul in Spain.**—But though St. James did not visit Spain, there is no good reason for doubting that *St. Paul* fulfilled his twice-expressed intention of preaching the Gospel in this country.* St. Clement, Bishop of Rome, who wrote about thirty years after the death of St. Paul, says that he "preached in the East and the West . . . having taught righteousness unto the whole world, and having reached the farthest bounds of the West."

At the time when he wrote this last expression would have been generally understood as referring to Spain. By the time that St. Paul reached Spain Roman civilization had spread throughout the country and Roman roads connected its principal towns. Tradition does not suggest that St. Paul founded any Churches in Spain, and it is doubtful whether any Christian communities existed there until a century later.

**The first Christian communities.**—It is probable that the first Christian communities were started by

* Rom. xv. 24–28 ; 2 Cor. i. 17.

Christians who came from Lyons in France. Irenæus, Bishop of Lyons, who died in 202, refers to the existence of a Church in Spain, and Tertullian, a little later, says that "all the confines of Spain have yielded to Christ." Arnobius, writing about 306, speaks of "innumerable" Christians in Spain, but his statement and that of Tertullian are probably not to be taken literally.

**Letter from Cyprian.**—The first definite and trustworthy statement relating to the existence of a Spanish Church occurs in a letter of Cyprian, bishop of Carthage, written in 258. It appears that two Spanish bishops, whose sees were at Leon-Astorga and Merida, had failed to act as confessors during an outbreak of persecution in 254, and had delivered to the Roman magistrate a certificate which implied that they had renounced their Christianity and had performed pagan rites. For this offence and for other alleged crimes they had been deposed and successors had been appointed, to whom, however, they had refused to give way. Stephen, the Bishop of Rome, supported the cause of the deposed bishops, but Cyprian, whose judgment was accepted by the Spanish Church, confirmed their deposition and secured the installation of their successors. From Cyprian's letter we gather that numerous Christian communities then existed in Spain, and that their bishops had already formed a synod of their own. We gather also that the character of the bishops was more worldly than was the case in Africa or elsewhere.

**Spanish martyrs.**—In the course of the next fifty years several Spanish Christians suffered martyrdom during the persecutions of Valerian, 256–260, and Diocletian, 303–304. It is, however, impossible to say how far the accounts of their martyrdoms are to be regarded as historical.

Bishop Prudentius, a Spanish bishop, who was born in 348, wrote fourteen poems in honour of these martyrs, thirty of whom, he says, suffered death during the

# HOW THE GOSPEL SPREAD

Diocletian persecution. The stern and fanatical spirit, which was so often exhibited in later time in Spain, characterized some of these early martyrs, who in many instances courted suffering and did everything in their power to provoke their persecutors to put them to death. Thus we read that Eulalia, a girl of thirteen, spat in the prætor's eyes and defied him to do his worst.

**St. Vincent.**—Vincent of Zaragoza, who was put to death at Saguntum, said to the prætor who was examining him, " The lightning shall burn thy poisonous tongue and thou shalt see the hot cinders of Gomorrah, and the ashes of Sodom shall witness thy everlasting burning. Thou serpent, whom the smoke of sulphur, and bitumen and pitch shall encircle in hell fire." Vincent is the most famous martyr whom Spain has produced, and the story of his martyrdom, interspersed with many miraculous occurrences, has spread far and wide. Thus St. Augustine in one of his sermons says, " What country, what province, to which the Roman Empire and the Christian name have been extended does not now rejoice to celebrate the festival of St. Vincent ? "

Four of the existing French cathedrals are dedicated to his memory.

**The Council of Elvira.**—One of the earliest Church councils which was held at Elvira near to the modern Granada about 306, was attended by nineteen bishops and twenty-six presbyters, who represented in all thirty-seven Christian communities in Spain. The decrees of this council, which have been preserved, although they throw little light upon missionary work, suggest that in many instances its results had been very superficial. They show, for example, that some even of the bishops and clergy lived immoral lives, and were addicted to pagan practices. Reference is made to Christians who were murderers, to parents who married their daughters to pagan priests, and to those who sacrificed to idols. Moreover there is reason to fear that the resolutions passed by the Council condemning the many evils to which they refer were not productive of great or lasting results. Sulpicius Severus, who wrote about a century later, gives an even more distressing account of the Spanish Church than that which is suggested by the decrees of this council.

**Monasteries.**—The first monasteries in Spain were established about the middle of the fourth century, but the clergy did not take kindly to the monastic system, and it was a long time before monasticism exerted as wide an influence as it did in some other countries.

**Bishop Hosius.**—The best known Spanish Christian during the fourth century was Hosius, bishop of Cordova, who was president of the council of Nicæa and lived to be over a hundred. By the end of the fourth century nearly the whole of the Spanish Peninsula had become nominally Christian, but of the missionaries to whose labours this result was due we know nothing, and it is unlikely that there were any individuals amongst them of outstanding mark.

**Invasion of Barbarians.**—In 409 a swarm of barbarians, Vandals, Suevi, and Alani, the first two of Germanic and the last of Scythian origin, burst through the passes of the Pyrenees and speedily overran the whole peninsula. The Vandals occupied Andalusia and Granada; the Suevi Galicia, Leon, and Castile; and the Alani Portugal and Estremadura. They were not, however, left long in the enjoyment of their conquests, as in 414 the Goths, under Atawulf, followed them into Spain. After defeating the Vandals and Alani, the Goths retired for a time to the district of Toulouse. The Suevi, who, apart from the Goths, formed the most important section of the Spanish population, embraced, together with their king Rekiar, an Arian form of Christianity in 438. In 466 the Goths completed their conquest of the peninsula, and by this time the earlier invaders had embraced Christianity. The Goths themselves were Arians, and a large part of the Spanish Christians remained Arians until the Gothic king, Recarred, who came to the throne in 586, renounced Arianism and became an orthodox Christian. His definite adhesion to orthodox Christianity was announced at the third Council of Toledo in 589.

Idolatry lingered on in some of the country districts for many years, and as late as the ninth century a temple of Mars and priests attached to it were to be found in a remote district to the north of the peninsula.

**The Moors.**—In 710 the Saracens, or Moors, as they were afterwards called, invaded Spain from Africa, and on July 19 of the following year, at the battle of Guadelete, the sovereignty of Spain passed from the Goths to the Moslems. Amongst those who sided with the invaders were the Jews, who had suffered much from the hands of their Christian rulers ; also the pagan slaves who became converts to Islam. Within three years the whole of Spain had become subject to the Moslems with the exception of the small district of Murcia, and the mountains of Asturias. The province of Narbonne in France, which was included in the Moslem conquests, was freed from their control as the result of the battle of Tours in 732.

To the inhabitants of Spain the Moslems offered the three alternatives of conversion to Islam, tribute, or the sword. Those who accepted the second alternative became known by the term Mozarabs. Most of these, although they did not accept Islam, became very indifferent Christians.

In 851 thirteen Christians suffered death as martyrs in Cordova, nearly all of whom had provoked the Moslems to attack them by reviling their prophet and their religion, and during the next few years about twenty suffered in a similar way. From the eleventh to the fifteenth century the history of Spain consists largely of wars waged, not only between Christians and Moslems, but between co-religionists on either side. As a result of these wars the Christians tended to become stronger in the north, especially in Castile, Galicia, Navarre, Aragon, and Portugal, but their internal dissensions prevented them from combining to drive out the Moslems from their country. Gradually, however, the Christians extended their conquests towards the south and by 1260 the rule of the Moslems was limited to the province of Granada in the extreme south. It was not till 1491 that the town of Granada surrendered to a Christian army.

**A Mission to Moslems.**—By the terms of its capitulation freedom of worship was guaranteed to the Moslems, and the first Christian archbishop, Hermando de Talavera, whilst respecting the terms granted to them, sought to promote their conversion to Christianity by sympathy and persuasion. With this end in view he ordered his clergy to learn Arabic, and he himself said his prayers in this language. So successful were his efforts that in 1499 three thousand Moslems were baptized in a single day. Had this unique missionary experiment been permitted to continue unchecked it is hard to say how great might have been its results. Unhappily, however, the policy of the archbishop failed to meet with the approval of his superiors. Cardinal Ximenes, who visited Granada at this time, disapproved of employing gentler means for the prosecution of missionary work when force was available, and persuaded the queen to issue a decree offering the Moslems the choice of baptism or exile.

**Compulsory conversions.**—To hasten their conversion still further, he closed their mosques and burnt countless manuscripts, which contained the results of Moslem study and learning.

As a result of the pressure exerted upon the Moslems a large number became nominal Christians, but their compulsory conversion caused them to hate everything connected with the Christian religion. They used to wash off the water with which their children had been baptized, and after a Christian wedding they returned to their homes to be married again with Moslem rites. In 1567

## 38  HOW THE GOSPEL SPREAD

Philip II. endeavoured to compel them to speak the Spanish language, to re-name themselves by Spanish names and to adopt Spanish dress. Soon afterwards a rebellion broke out which lasted for two years, and was repressed with barbarous cruelty, and in 1570, when the Moslems were finally subdued, the survivors were either sold as slaves or exiled, the deportation of the last remnant taking place in 1610. The methods by which the Moslems were finally subdued and the results which ensued are summarized by Lane Poole in his history of the Moors in Spain. He writes: "The (Spanish) Grand Commander Requesens by an organized system of wholesale butchery and devastation, by burning down villages, and smoking the people to death in the caves where they had sought refuge, extinguished the last spark of open revolt before November 5, 1570. The Moriscos were at last subdued at the cost of the honour, and with the loss of the future of Christian Spain. . . . The Moors were banished; for a while Christian Spain shone, like the moon, with a borrowed light; then came the eclipse, and in that darkness Spain has grovelled ever since."

**The Jews in Spain.**—We have not space in which to refer to the efforts that were made from time to time to bring about the forcible conversion of Jews in Spain. In no country were these efforts accompanied by such barbarous cruelty or by such wholesale massacres of those who refused to be baptized. In one instance a Dominican monk named Vincent Lerrer, who lived at the beginning of the fifteenth century, protested against these cruelties, and by himself adopting methods of kindness and persuasion he is said to have secured the voluntary conversion of many thousands of Jews.*

* For an account of the treatment of the Jews in the different countries of Europe, and the attempts made by Christians to secure their conversion, see "The Conversion of Europe," pp. 536–570.

Happy would it have been for Spain if his methods had been endorsed by the representatives of the Spanish Church, and if the pages of its history had never been disfigured by the horrors of the Spanish Inquisition.

## V

## FRANCE

**EARLY legends.**—Early legends, which have, however, no historical value, assert that the first missionaries to France, or Gaul, as it was then called, included several whose names are mentioned in the New Testament; for example, Mary Magdalene, Lazarus, Dionysius the Areopagite, and Trophimus the companion of St. Paul. We do not know how the Gospel was first preached in this country, but we know that by the year 177 Christian Churches existed at Lyons and Vienne, the latter being a town on the river Rhone a few miles below Lyons.

**Martyrs at Lyons.**—In this year a fierce persecution broke out, and forty-eight martyrs suffered death rather than deny their faith. Of these at least three had come from Asia Minor, and the majority of the rest bore Greek names and were probably Greeks. Amongst the martyrs was *Pothinus*, the aged Bishop of Lyons. When the bishop, who was ninety years of age, was placed before the Roman judge he was asked by him who was the God of the Christians. He replied, "If thou art worthy thou shalt know." Two days later he died as the result of the ill-treatment to which he had been subjected. Another martyr whose name became celebrated was the servant-maid *Blandina*. She remained constant under long-continued tortures, and, after being tossed by wild bulls, was at last killed by the blow of an executioner. One of the survivors was *Irenaeus*, the priest of Lyons, who had been ordained priest by Pothinus, and was afterwards consecrated by the Bishop of Rome as the second Bishop of

Lyons. His episcopate connects the Gallic Church with the immediate successors of the apostles, for, as he tells us, when staying with Polycarp at Smyrna he had heard him describe to the Christians at Smyrna his intercourse with St. John and with others who had seen the Lord.

The account of these martyrdoms is contained in a letter which has come down to us and which was written by some of the surviving Christians in order to let their fellow-Christians in Asia Minor know what had befallen their brethren. Though the account tells us nothing concerning the missionaries who had brought a knowledge of the faith to the inhabitants of Lyons and Vienne, it provides evidence that the work done by them had been effective. Irenæus preached in Celtic as well as in Greek, but, up to the beginning of the third century, Greek was the language spoken by educated people in the south of France, and most of the early Christians there probably spoke Greek.

*Saturninus*, who was bishop of Toulouse about 250, suffered death as a martyr. According to the story of his martyrdom, which is probably founded on fact, Saturninus, who had for some time preached against the idolatry of the people of Toulouse, was seized by them on the occasion of an idol festival, and tied to a bull that was being led out for sacrifice. When bidden by the people to offer sacrifice to the gods, he replied, " I know the one true God and will offer to Him the sacrifices of praise : your gods I know to be demons." He was then fastened by his feet to the bull, and after being dragged through the street died of the injuries that he had received.

The author of the service which was afterwards held in commemoration of his martyrdom writes : " The sound of the Gospel stole out gradually and by degrees into all the earth, and the preaching of the apostles shone throughout our country with but a slow progress, since only a few Churches in some of the states, and these containing but few Christians, stood up together in their devotion to their religion.

Another missionary who lived about the same time was *Gatianus*, the first bishop of Tours. Gregory, who became Bishop of Tours 300 years later and wrote a history of the Franks, says of him, " In the first year of the Emperor Decius (249) Gatian was sent by the Bishop of Rome as the first bishop (of Tours), in which city lived a multitude of pagans who were devoted to idolatry, some of whom he converted to the Lord by his preaching. But at times he concealed himself owing to the hostility of those in power . . . and in caverns and hiding-places, together with the few Christians who had been converted by him, he was wont to celebrate secretly the Holy Mystery, and in this city under these conditions he lived for forty years and died in peace."

In 313 the Edict of Milan, which was issued by the Emperors Constantine and Licinius, put an end to religious persecution, and in France, as elsewhere, many enrolled themselves as Christians who made little attempt to lead a Christian life. The extent to which the organization of the Church in France had been developed at this period may be seen from the fact that at the Council of Arles, held in the following year, in order to decide a controversy that had arisen among the Christians in North Africa, twelve bishops from the province of Gaul were present who represented almost every part of what is now France.

**Martin of Tours.**—The first great missionary in France of whose work we have any satisfactory information was *Martin*, who became Bishop of Tours in 372. He was a native of Hungary, and served for a time as a soldier in the Imperial army. We are fortunate to possess a life of him written by a friend named Sulpicius Severus, who had known him intimately, and though the writer of his life devotes an undue proportion of his space to records of miracles which he attributes to Martin, what he tells us of Martin's character and work is of great

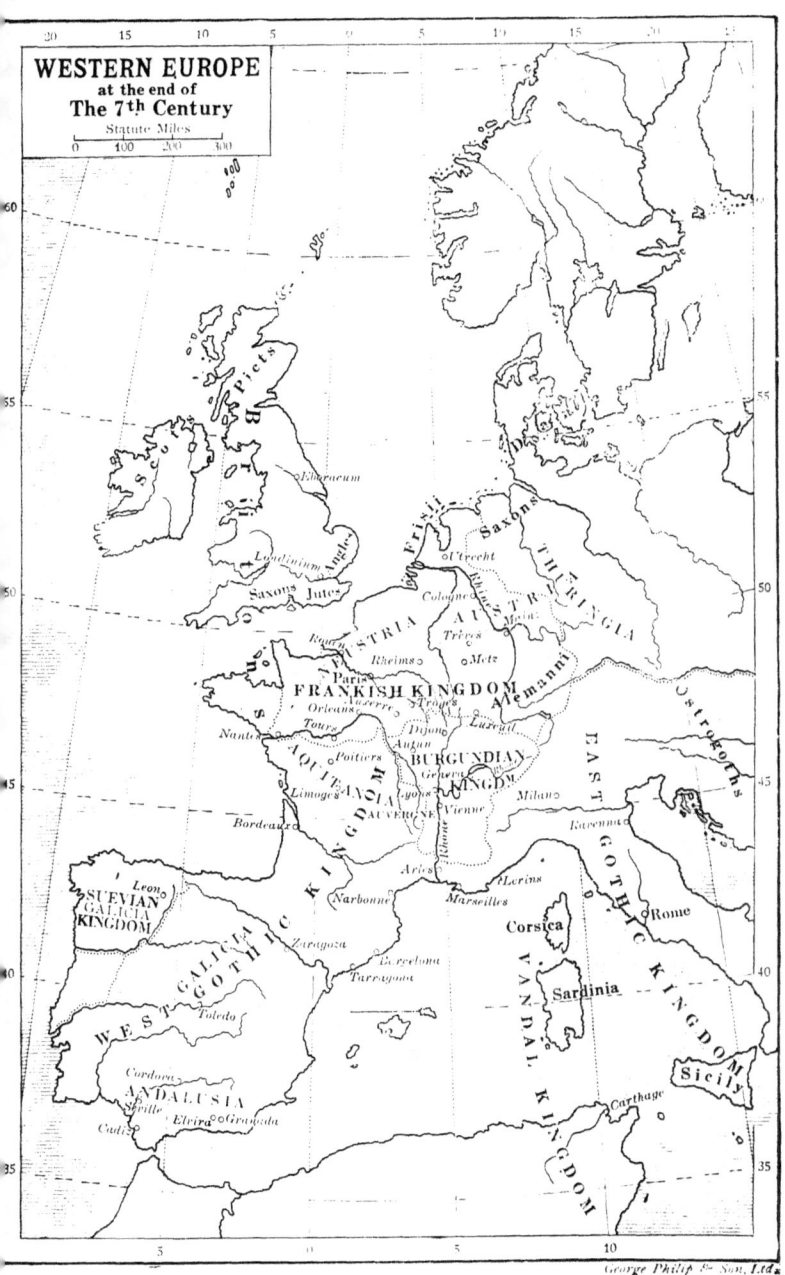

value. One of the best known stories relating to his life, before he became a bishop, is told thus by Sulpicius.

Noticing a beggar at the gate of the city of Amiens who was ill-clad and suffering from the cold, Martin, who had no money to give, drew his sword, and, cutting his military cloak in two, gave half to the beggar. The same night Christ appeared to him in a vision clad in the half of the coat that he had given to the beggar, and said to the angels who stood with Him, "Martin, still a catechumen, covered Me with this robe." Soon afterwards, at the age of eighteen, he was baptized.

A few years after he had obtained his discharge from the Roman army, Martin founded a monastery at Poitiers which, together with the monastery that he afterwards founded at Marmoutier near Tours, became the training home of many missionaries to whom the evangelization of France was due. From Poitiers and Tours as centres of work Martin evangelized a large part of central France. The following are a few incidents which are related by his biographer Sulpicius.

At Chartres, the pagan people were induced to abandon their idols and accept the Christian faith after witnessing the restoration to life of a dead man as the result of Martin's prayers. At a village called Leprosum, where the people had resisted his attempts to destroy their richly endowed temple, Martin, having sat by the temple for three days in sackcloth and ashes, secured by his prayers the help of two angels whose appearance influenced the people to allow the destruction of their temple and idols and eventually resulted in their conversion to the faith. In another village, after Martin had set fire to an ancient and celebrated temple, the flames began to spread to an adjacent house, but were miraculously stayed by his intervention. Whatever credence we may give to the miraculous powers said to have been exercised by Martin, the above incidents, recorded, as they were, by a contemporary writer, testify to his missionary zeal, and to his success in uprooting pagan worship.

On many different occasions he took a leading part in the destruction of idols or heathen temples, and in several instances the people to whom he preached destroyed these at his instigation, and erected in their places churches for Christian worship. To quote a single instance out of the many that are recorded by Sulpicius : " There was in a certain village (apparently in Burgundy) an ancient temple and a tree which was regarded as specially sacred. Although the pagans had consented to the destruction of the temple, they refused to allow Martin to cut down the tree. At length one of them suggested that if the bishop believed in the power of his God to protect him he should stand on the spot where the tree was likely to fall, while he and his companions cut it down. Martin accepted the proposal with alacrity, and stood on the spot suggested by the pagans. When the tree fell, it fell amongst the people and left Martin standing unhurt." The impression made upon the inhabitants of this district was so great that a large number of them were shortly afterwards baptized. Concerning Martin's personal character his biographer writes : " No one ever saw him enraged or excited, or lamenting or laughing : he was always one and the same, displaying a kind of heavenly happiness in his countenance, he seemed to have passed the ordinary limits of human nature. Never was there any word on his lips but Christ." Again, referring to his humility, he writes : " When sitting in his retirement he never used a chair, and as to the church, no one ever saw him sitting there, as I recently saw a certain man, not without a feeling of shame at the spectacle, seated on a lofty throne . . . but Martin might be seen sitting on a rude little three-legged stool."

If Martin's success as a missionary and a teacher was in part due to his humility, it was at least equally due to his prayerfulness. Thus we read in his biography, " never did a single hour or moment pass in which he was not either actually engaged in prayer, or, if it happened that he was occupied with something else, still he never let his mind loose from prayer." It would have been a miracle greater than any of those in which his biography abounds if his unceasing prayers had been unproductive of far-reaching results. Another point on which his biographer lays special stress was his belief in the reality and the constant presence of good and evil spirits. Martin constantly asserted that not only saints who had lived in the past, but the devil and his angels, appeared in bodily form and conversed with him. It may well have been that his success as a missionary was partly due to the fact that the victories which he believed himself to have won over the powers of evil during his long hours of prayer gave him the assurance of divine support which was the immediate cause of his missionary triumphs amongst his heathen neighbours.

**Martin's Visions.**—The most celebrated of Martin's visions is that in which the devil appeared to him clad in royal apparel, and, with golden sandals on his feet, asked from him the homage due to Christ.

"Recognize," said Martin's visitor, "whom you look upon. I am Christ, and I have come down to earth to reveal myself to you." As Martin, dazzled by his appearance, preserved a long silence, he added, "Acknowledge, O Martin, who it is that you behold. I am Christ, and, being about to descend to the earth, I desired first to manifest myself to thee." Martin continued silent, whereupon his visitor continued, "Why do you hesitate to believe when you see? I am Christ." Then Martin replied, "The Lord Jesus did not predict that He would come clad in purple and with a glittering diadem on His head. I will not believe that Christ has come unless He wears that garb and form in which He suffered and displays before me the marks of His passion." On hearing this his visitor vanished, and Martin knew that he had been speaking to the devil. Sulpicius states that he heard this story from Martin's own mouth.

In whatever way we explain this and the other visions attributed to Martin, they afford us an insight into his character, and help us to understand how real for him was the conflict between the powers of good and evil in which he was engaged.

**Invasion by Barbarians.**—On December 31, 406, that is sixteen years after the death of Martin, an army of Vandals, Alans and Sueves, all of whom were pagans, crossed the Rhine and began to invade Gaul. As they advanced westwards they massacred a large part of the population, and spread ruin and desolation around them. In, or about, 411 A.D. *Patrick*, who had recently escaped from his captivity in Ireland, landed, probably at the mouth of the River Loire, in order to reach Italy *viâ* Aquitaine. In his Confessions he speaks of wandering across country which had been deprived of all means of subsistence, and during a whole month's travel he seems only once to have met with any remaining trace of civilization.

Jerome (in 409), referring to Aquitaine, says that as a result of this invasion in the four provinces of Lyons and the two of Narbonne there were but few cities left with any inhabitants. As for Toulouse he could not mention it without shedding tears. In a poem attributed to Prosper of Aquitaine the writer declares that if the entire ocean had been poured out upon the fields of Gaul the destruction would not have been so complete as was that wrought by these invaders.

In 451 the Huns under Attila devastated a large part of Eastern Gaul, but after being defeated near Orleans, retired again across the Rhine.

**Baptism of Clovis.**—In 493, Clovis, king of the Franks, who had married a Christian princess Hrothilde, a daughter of the Burgundian king Hilperik, having, as he believed, secured success in one of his campaigns as a result of praying to Hrothilde's God, decided to become a Christian. His baptism, the date of which forms a landmark in the spread of Christianity in Northern Europe, took place at Rheims on Christmas Day 496. When Bishop Remigius was about to administer the sacrament of baptism, he said to the king : " Bow thy neck in humility, O Sicambrian ; accept as an object of worship that which thou wast wont to destroy, and burn that which once thou worshipped."

**Columbanus.**—The next great missionary in France after the time of Martin was the Irish saint Columbanus, who was born in West Leinster in 543, and was educated at Bangor monastery near Belfast. He crossed to Brittany with twelve companions about 573, and after labouring there for some time presented himself before Sigibert of Austrasia, and asked his permission to settle in some barren and uncared-for district in Gaul, the north-eastern portion of which had suffered terribly from the irruption of barbarian invaders. The spot in which Columbanus and his companions settled lies on the western side of the Vosges mountains, in what was then called the Jura district, and near the old Roman camp of Anagrates (in Haute-Saone). They could have found no wilder or less inviting district, and for a considerable time they suffered pangs of hunger and were in danger of starvation ; but, despite the hardships that they had to endure, their number continued to increase, and after a few years they built a much larger monastery at Luxeuil, eight miles further south. At the time when Columbanus settled in France by far the greater part of the country had become nominally Christian, but the condition of the so-called Christian Church was deplorable. Bishops, who were in some cases laymen, who had never been consecrated as bishops, regarded their dioceses as private estates, and bequeathed them to their friends or relations. Many of them lived as laymen, and spent their lives in fighting, hunting, and revelry. The result was the total demoralisation of the Frankish Church in northern Gaul, a demoralization which was accentuated by the evil lives of the Frankish kings, who were nominally Christians.

It is not to be wondered at that Columbanus and his fellow-missionaries, who had been accustomed to a life of rigid asceticism and self-control, refused to place the monasteries which they founded under the control of the Frankish bishops. Their aim was not only to convert the heathen, but, by their lives and teaching, to wage war upon the kind of Christianity which they found existing in France. Unfortunately the very aloofness from their fellow-churchmen which they maintained limited their spiritual influence and prevented them from acting as reformers of the evils by which the Church was afflicted. Although Columbanus refused to place his monasteries, or missionaries, under the control of the bishops, he treated them with the respect due to their high office. Thus in a letter addressed by him to a Frankish synod (in 602) which had remonstrated with him for not conforming to Gallic Church customs, he wrote—

" I came as a stranger amongst you on behalf of our common Lord and Master Jesus Christ. In His name I beseech you let me live in peace and quiet, as I have lived for twelve years in these woods beside the bones of my seventeen departed brethren. Let Gaul receive into her bosom all who, if they deserve it, will meet in one heaven. . . . Choose ye which rule respecting Easter ye prefer to follow, remembering the words of the Apostle, ' Prove all things; hold fast that which is good.' But let us not quarrel one with another, lest our enemies, the Jews, the heretics and pagan Gentiles rejoice in our contention. . . . Pray for us, my fathers, even as we, humble as we are, pray for you. Regard us not as strangers, for we are members together of one body, whether we be Gauls, or Britons, or Iberians, or to whatever nation we belong. Therefore, let us all rejoice in the knowledge of the faith and the revelation of the Son of God in communion with whom let us learn to love one another and pray for one another."

His attitude, and that of his fellow-missionaries, towards those from whom they differed is one which might with advantage be copied by all missionaries in the world to-day. The work of Columbanus at Luxeuil was cut short in 610 by Theodoric, the young king of the Burgundians, whose immoral life he had frequently rebuked. The king caused him to be put on board a boat at Nantes which was sailing for Ireland; but, the boat having met with a violent storm, the captain disembarked Columbanus and his four companions.

**Columbanus at Lake Zurich.**—He then proceeded to Lake Zurich and worked for a while as a missionary, in company with another Irishman named Gall, amongst the heathen Alemanni and Suevi. His Irish impetuosity and that of his companion rendered it difficult for him to gain the goodwill of the heathen or to commend to them his faith. Two incidents described by his biographer suggest that he had failed to understand the direction given by our Lord to His first missionaries that in preaching the Gospel they were to be " wise as serpents." When the Alemanni produced a barrel containing ten gallons of beer which they proposed to drink in his honour, Columbanus, if we may accept the statement made by his biographer, breathed upon the barrel, with the result that it forthwith burst asunder with a loud crash. We do not wonder that the Alemanni rejected the message of the missionaries and forced them to depart. On leaving the Lake of Zurich they settled at Bregenz, where they found the ruins of what had once been a Christian chapel, to the walls of which were affixed three brazen images. " These images," said the people, " are our ancient gods, by whose help and comfort we have been preserved alive to this day." Gall, the companion of Columbanus, who was able to speak to the people in their own language, urged them to abandon the worship of these idols, and to serve the true God. Then, in the sight of all the people, Columbanus seized the idols, battered them into fragments, and threw the pieces into the lake. The hostility aroused by this act led to the murder of two of the missionaries, and caused Columbanus to seek a new sphere of work. We have already referred to his arrival in Italy and to his death at Bobbio in 615.

**Columbanus and the Pope.**—Although Columbanus on several occasions expressed respect for the office held by the Bishop of Rome, he started his missionary work in Gaul entirely on his own initiative, and did not visit Rome until after he had left Gaul. He was far from being a believer in Papal infallibility, and was quite ready to criticize the bishops of Rome when he thought them mistaken. Thus, in one of his letters to Pope Gregory relating to the time of the observance of Easter, he urges the Pope not to feel bound by the decrees of his predecessor, St. Leo, on the ground that a living dog is better than a dead lion (leo), and suggests that a living saint may correct the omissions of one who went before him. In another letter addressed to Boniface IV., shortly before his own death, he writes: "We Irish who inhabit the extremities of the world are the disciples of St. Peter and St. Paul, and of the other apostles who have written under dictation of the Holy Spirit. We receive nothing more than the apostolic and evangelical doctrine. . . . Pardon me if . . . I have said some words offensive to pious ears. The native liberty of my race has given me that boldness. With us it is not the person, it is right which prevails."

With an ardent faith and a readiness to endure privations and trials he combined a spirit of angry impatience which his biographer does not attempt to conceal. Thus, on the occasion when the people on Lake Zurich refused to listen to his preaching he invoked maledictions upon them in these words: "Make this generation to be a reproach that the evils which they have wickedly devised for Thy servants they may feel on their own heads. Let their children perish, and when they come to middle age let stupefaction and madness seize upon them."

Columbanus was an Irishman, and if the impetuosity which is characteristic of his race caused him to do or say things which ill became a Christian missionary, it led him also to attempt enterprises which might have been regarded by others as forlorn hopes.

**The Celtic missionaries in Europe.**—In estimating the influence which Columbanus and the other Celtic missionaries exerted on the continent of Europe we must give them the credit for having raised the standard of learning in Gaul, and for having inspired monks and clergy alike with the desire to study the Scriptures, and in addition the Latin and Greek classics. It was a common saying in the days of Charles the Bald (823–77), that any one on the Continent who knew Greek was an Irishman or had obtained his knowledge from an Irishman. The Celtic missionaries were as a rule men of good education, and their training included not only the Scriptures and early Christian writers, but the ancient classics. The writings of Columbanus show that he was acquainted with Virgil and other Latin authors, and several of the Irish who devoted themselves to missionary work were the authors of treatises on grammar and rhetoric.

The study, however, of ancient languages and literature was ever regarded by them as a means whereby to obtain a more perfect understanding of the Holy Scriptures. It is doubtful whether any missionaries of modern times have regarded an intimate acquaintance with the Scriptures as of more vital consequence for the prosecution of their work than did these early monkish students.

By the time that Columbanus had finished his work in France, the whole of the country had become nominally Christian. Several centuries, however, had still to elapse before paganism was completely abolished or even the public observance of heathen ceremonies entirely disappeared.

**Hardships of the early missionaries.**—The work of the early missionaries was carried on under circumstances of which it is hard for us to form any conception. At the period when their missionary labours were accomplished, the greater part of France, and, indeed, the greater part of Europe, consisted of forests inhabited by numerous wild beasts, infested in many districts by still fiercer brigands, and as difficult to traverse as is any Central African forest to-day. "To plunge into these terrible forests, to encounter these monstrous animals . . . required a courage of which nothing in the existing world can give us an idea. . . . The monk attacked these gloomy woods without arms, without sufficient implements, and often without a single companion. . . . He bore with him a strength which nothing has ever surpassed or equalled, the strength conferred by faith in a living God. . . . See, then, these men of prayer and penitence who were at the same time the bold pioneers of Christian civilization and the modern world. . . . They plunged into the darkness carrying light with them, a light which was nevermore to be extinguished." \*

\* "The Monks of the West," ii. 320.

## VI

## IRELAND

IRELAND has an interest from a missionary point of view which no other country in Europe can claim to possess.

In the first place it can claim to have been the only country which has never had a Christian martyr; the Christian faith was accepted by its people without any outbreak or persecution which resulted in the death of a missionary or other Christian.

**Irish missionaries on the Continent.**—In the second place, Ireland has a special claim upon our attention because the Irish did more for the evangelization of Europe than did the representatives of any other land. There was hardly any country in northern or central Europe which did not share in the spiritual blessings which Ireland's sons helped to confer upon the continent of Europe with lavish hands, and during a long series of years. In speaking of the work of Columbanus in France we have already referred to the deep and wide-spread influence which the Irish missionaries exerted in that country, and we shall have occasion to refer later on to their missionary labours in Scandinavia, Denmark, the Netherlands, and Germany.

**The introduction of Christianity.**—Of the beginning of Christianity in Ireland we know nothing. The Roman coins that have been found, and which date back to the first century, suggest that trade communications between Ireland and Italy existed in very early times, and it is possible that a knowledge of the Christian faith was first introduced by Christian traders. All that we know for certain is that some time before 431 Christianity had begun to spread throughout the island.

**Palladius.**—A French writer named Prosper of Aquitaine, who wrote in 431, says that Pope Celestine sent a bishop called Palladius to the Irish who believed in Christ. A later tradition asserts that Palladius died a short time after his arrival in Ireland.

**St. Patrick.**—Ireland's greatest missionary, who afterwards became her patron saint, was Patrick. Many questions have arisen in regard to his work, to which no certain replies can be given, but we fortunately possess two works written by Patrick himself which tell us in his own words a good deal about himself. These works are his Confession, and a letter addressed by him to a king named Coroticus in North Britain.

From these writings we learn the following facts. His father, Calpornius, who was a Roman decurio, was in deacon's orders, and his grandfather Potitus was a priest. His father owned a small farm near a village called Bannaven Taberniæ, which was probably at Dumbarton in Scotland.\* In his sixteenth year he was carried captive with several others to Ireland, and for six years was employed by his master in herding swine. Before he was carried captive he had thought little about religion, but in his trouble he learned to pray. Thus he writes: "After I had come to Ireland I daily used to feed swine, and I prayed frequently during the day; the love of God and the fear of Him increased more and more, and faith became stronger, and the spirit was stirred, so that in one day I said about a hundred prayers, and in the night nearly the same, so that I used even to remain in the woods and in the mountains; before daylight I used to rise to prayer, through snow, through frost,

---

\* Professor Bury maintains that it was situated on the Bristol Channel. See "Conversion of Europe," p. 50.

through rain, and felt no harm." The habit and power of prayer which he thus acquired, when hardly more than a boy, go far towards explaining the spiritual influence which he exerted in later life.

In his Confession he refers to an offence that he had committed when he was fifteen years old, which was brought up against him in later life. He writes: "I did not believe in the one God from my infancy, but I remained in death and unbelief until I was severely chastised. . . . Before I was humbled I was like a stone lying in deep mud." It is hardly necessary to point out that these statements conflict with the later traditions which tell of the exceptional piety of his early days. At the end of six years his longing to return to his native land was enhanced by a vision in which he heard a voice telling him that the ship in which he was to escape was waiting for him. He accordingly left his master, and, after a walk of about two hundred miles, reached a port. Part of the cargo of the boat in which he sailed consisted of dogs, probably Irish wolf-hounds, and after three days at sea he reached land on the coast of Gaul. On leaving the boat he and his companions, accompanied by their dogs, travelled for twenty-eight days through a desert, or a deserted country, where they suffered greatly from hunger. When food failed, the leader of the party, a heathen, appealed to Patrick for help, and said to him, "What is it, O Christian? You say that thy God is great and almighty; why, therefore, canst thou not pray for us, for we are perishing with hunger." "I said to them plainly," writes Patrick, "turn with faith to the Lord my God, to whom nothing is impossible, that He may send food this day for us in your path, even till you are satisfied, for it abounds everywhere with Him." The appearance of a herd of swine, which immediately followed, was regarded by Patrick and his companions as an answer to his prayers. A statement to the effect that after many years he was taken captive once more, which is here abruptly inserted in his Confession, is apparently to be interpreted as a reference to the spiritual compulsion which forced him to become a missionary to the land in which he had been a captive in his youth. Again, "after a few years," but while still young, he was at his home, "in the Britains," where his parents (*i.e.* probably relations) begged him to remain. "There," he writes, " I saw in the bosom of the night, a man coming as it were from Ireland, Victoricus by name, with innumerable letters, and he gave one of them to me. And I read the beginning of the letter containing 'The voice of the Irish.' And while I was reading aloud the beginning of the letter, I myself thought indeed in my mind that I heard the voice of those who were near the wood of Foclut, which is close by the Western Sea. And they cried out thus as if with one voice, 'We entreat thee, holy youth, that thou come and henceforth walk among us.' And I was deeply moved in heart, and could read no further, and so I awoke." In another vision he heard a voice which said, " He who gave His life for thee is He who speaks to thee." Here, unfortunately, his own record abruptly ends, but from the latter part of his Confession and his letter to Coroticus we glean the following additional details :—

Before or after this vision he spent some time in Gaul, in which country were some whom he had learned to regard as his brethren. When he was almost worn out he went, or returned, to Ireland as a missionary, where, on twelve separate occasions, his life was imperilled, and where he says, it has "come to pass that they who never had any knowledge and until now have only worshipped idols and unclean things, have lately become a people of the Lord and are called the sons of God. Sons of the Scots (Irish) and daughters of chieftains are seen to be monks and virgins of Christ." Having been consecrated as a bishop (apparently in Gaul) he ordained clergy in many different places and baptized many thousands of men.

The clergy whom he ordained included one whom he had taught from his infancy. Having come to Ireland as a missionary, he felt "bound by the spirit" not to see again any of his kindred.

On the twelve occasions on which his life was imperilled, "the most holy God" delivered him. Those to whom his Confession, which was written in his old age, was addressed were "witnesses that the Gospel has been preached everywhere in places where there is no man beyond."

The above is all the information relating to Patrick's missionary work of which we can be reasonably certain. Traditions, which date from several centuries later, assert that he visited Rome and received a commission from the Pope, and that he performed during his stay in Ireland a long succession of miracles, but his own writings give no support to these traditions. The date of his arrival in Ireland as a bishop was 432, and the date of his death was probably 461. A hymn, called the Lorica, or Breastplate, which was probably written by Patrick, contains a beautiful amplification of the statement of St. Paul, "I live, and yet no longer I, but Christ liveth in me." The author of the hymn writes:

> "Christ with me, Christ before me,
> Christ behind me, Christ in me,
> Christ under me, Christ over me,
> Christ to right of me, Christ to left of me,
> Christ in lying down, Christ in sitting, Christ in rising up."

Patrick's statement that "sons of the Scots (Irish) and daughters of chieftains are seen to be monks and virgins of Christ," suggests that he was the means of establishing, and perhaps of introducing, monasteries throughout Ireland. The early monasteries and monastic schools were collections of rude huts made of planks and moss, and the church which was attached, being built of wood, frequently bore the name Duirthech, that is "house of oak." Many of these were situated on islands round the coast or in the inland lochs.

From these monasteries or their successors went forth a stream of missionaries who won for Ireland her fame both as the Isle of Saints and as the greatest of all centres of missionary zeal and activity.

Tradition asserts that before Patrick died there were at least three other bishops in Ireland, but of their missionary labours we know nothing.

**St. Bridget.**—The life and work of Bridget are lost in a mist of tradition, and it is not quite certain that she ever existed. She is said to have been baptized by a disciple of Patrick and to have become the foundress of a large number of religious communities for women. There are eighteen places in Ireland called Kilbrid, a name which denotes church of Bridget.

In the sixth century there was apparently a pagan reaction throughout a great part of Ireland, and in the early part of the ninth century the Danes established the worship of Thor at Armagh and endeavoured to eradicate Christianity, but ere long they became subject to Christian influences and paganism finally disappeared.

## VII

## SCOTLAND

THE country to which the first Irish missionaries directed their steps is clearly visible from the north coast of Ireland, and its western shores were inhabited by men of the same race as themselves.

**The word "Scots."**—The names "Scot" and "Scotia" were in early times used only of the Irish and of Ireland, and up to the twelfth century the word "Scots" was employed to denote alike the Irish in Ireland and the Irish settlers on the west coast of Scotland. Christianity had reached Scotland before any missionaries from Ireland, of whom we have any knowledge, had set foot on its shores.

**St. Ninian.**—The first missionary concerning whom we have any trustworthy information is Ninian. Born of Christian parents on the shores of the Solway about 350, he is said to have been consecrated as a bishop in Rome, and to have visited Martin at Tours on his way back to Scotland. From him he procured masons, by whose help he afterwards built a "church of stone." He laboured as a missionary amongst the southern Picts who inhabited the middle parts of Scotland south of the Grampians. The Picts, who were converted by Ninian, had apparently relapsed into heathenism by the middle of the sixth century, when another missionary, named Kentigern, or St. Mungo, as he is commonly called in Scotland, appeared in their midst.

**Kentigern.**—Of Kentigern we know even less than we know of Ninian. If we may credit a life of him written in the twelfth century, he was chosen as bishop of Strathclyde when he was twenty-five, and later on established a monastery at Glasgow, where he remained till the hostility of a new king of Strathclyde forced him to leave Scotland. In the course of his journey south he preached in the districts near Carlisle, where to-day there are nine churches dedicated to his memory. After visiting Bishop David in Wales he returned to Glasgow on the invitation of a new king named Roderick. The date of his death was about 603.

**Columba.**—We pass on now to Scotland's greatest missionary and saint, Columba. Born in Donegal in 521, he was educated at the monastic school at Movilla, and, having been ordained a priest, he devoted fifteen years to founding monasteries and churches in various parts of Ireland. According to a tradition, which is, however, of uncertain value, his departure from Ireland was the result of a dispute that arose between him and his former teacher Finnian of Movilla in regard to the possession of a Gospel, or Psalter, which Columba had copied out. The judgment delivered by the king of Meath, to whom the dispute was referred, was, "To every cow her calf belongs, and so to every book its child-book." Columba, enraged at the decision, invited his kinsmen to wage war against the supporters of Finnian, and in the battle that ensued 3000 men were killed. As an act of reparation for the slaughter which he had caused, Columba decided to devote his life to missionary work amongst the Picts until he had converted to Christ as many persons as had been killed in this battle, but whether this tradition be true or not it is impossible to say.

**Iona.**—In 563, he landed on Iona off the west coast of Scotland, together with a few companions, and proceeded to build a church and some monastic cells. Of his work amongst the Picts on the mainland his biographers have preserved no details. The greater part of the thirty-four years which elapsed after his departure from Ireland were spent in Iona, where he lived a life of prayer and self-denial, and where he laid the foundations of what proved to be an important centre of missionary enterprise.

**Columba's intercessory prayers.**—An illustration of the influence which Columba exercised by his intercessory prayers on behalf of his fellow-workers is afforded by the beautiful story by Adamnan, his first biographer. He writes : " As the Brethren, after harvest work, were returning to the monastery in the evening . . . they seemed each one to feel within himself something wonderful and unusual . . . and for some days at the same place, and at the same hour in the evening, they perceived it. . . . One of them, a senior (when asked to explain) says . . . ' a certain and unaccustomed and incomparable joy spread abroad in my heart, which of a sudden consoles me in a wonderful way, and so greatly gladdens me that I can think neither of sadness nor labour. The load, moreover, however heavy, which I am carrying on my back from this place until we come to the monastery, is so much lightened, how I know not, that I do not feel that I am bearing any burden.' When all the others had made similar statements, Baithene, ' the superintendent of labours among them,' said, ' Ye know that Columba, mindful of our toil, thinks anxiously about us and grieves that we come to him so late, and by reason that he comes not in body to meet us, his spirit meets our steps, and that is it which so much consoles and makes us glad.' "

Referring to his life of continuous devotion and labour, he writes again, " He could not pass the space even of a single hour without applying himself either to prayer, or reading, or writing, or also to some manual labour. By day and by night he was so occupied, without any intermission, in unwearied exercise of fasts and vigils that the burden of any one of these particular labours might seem to be beyond human endurance. And, amid all, dear to all, ever showing a pleasant holy countenance he was gladdened in his inmost heart by the joy of the Holy Spirit."

**Columba's character.**—From the life of Adamnan we gather that Columba possessed the first and greatest qualification of a teacher and trainer of missionaries, viz. the power of sympathy. The ascetic life which he himself lived did not render him incapable of entering into the feelings and aspirations of others, or cause him to hold aloof from those whose temperament was different from his own. Thus Bishop Westcott writes: " Columba loved men, and through love he understood them. He was enabled to recognize the signs of a divine kinsmanship, the unconscious strivings after noble things, in the ignorant, the rude, the wayward. . . . By a living sympathy he entered into the souls of those who came before him. He had mastered the secret of effective help to the suffering by making his own the burden of which they could be relieved. Columba loved men and he loved nature, because in both he saw God. His vision embraced the great spiritual realities of life. He regarded things with a spiritual eye ; therefore his countenance flashed from time to time with beams of an unearthly joy, when, in the language of his biographer, he saw the ministering angels round about him."

The humility and gentleness which he displayed when settled in Iona render it difficult for us to credit the tradition that he had raised an army in Ireland to avenge a personal affront ; though it is not impossible that a son of thunder may have been transformed into an apostle of love. Another and later biographer of Columba, by way of illustrating his humility and piety, writes : " He would bathe the feet of the Brethren after their daily labour, he would carry the bags of flour from the mill to the kitchen, he subjected himself to great austerities, sleeping on a hide spread on the ground with a stone for a pillow, being most strict and constant in fasting, in prayer, in meditation."

**Death of Columba.**—Adamnan's description of "the passing away" of the saint is worth quoting at some length. Knowing that the end was near at hand, "the old man, weary with age, is borne on a waggon and goes to visit the Brethren while at their work." To them he says: "During the Easter festival . . . with desire I have desired to pass away to Christ, . . . but lest a festival of joy should be turned for you into sadness, I thought it better to put off the day of my departure from the world a little longer." Then "sitting just as he was in the waggon, turning his face eastward, he blessed the island, with its inhabitants." At the end of the same week he and his attendant, Diormit, went to bless the granary, and he gave thanks to God for the store of corn which it contained. As he was returning from the granary, "a white horse, the same that used, as a willing servant, to carry the milk vessels from the cowshed to the monastery, runs up to him, and lays his head against his breast . . . and knowing that his master was soon about to leave him, and that he would see him no more, began to whinny and to shed copious tears into the lap of the saint." Columba refused to allow the horse to be interfered with, and "he blessed his servant, the horse, as it sadly turned to go away from him." Then he ascended a little hill which overlooked the monastery, and after standing for a while on the top he raised both his hands and blessed the monastery, saying, "Upon this place, small though it be and mean, not only the kings of the Scots (Irish) and their peoples, but also the rulers of barbarous and foreign races, with the people subject to them, shall confer great and notable honour: by the saints also even of other churches shall no common reverence be accorded to it." Returning again to the monastery he sat in his hut transscribing the thirty-fourth psalm, and when he came to the verse, "They that seek the Lord shall not want any good thing," he said, "I must stop at the foot of this page, and what follows let Baithene write." Then he attended vespers in the church, and afterwards, sitting up in his cell, he addressed his last words to the Brethren, saying, "These my last words I commend to you, O my sons, that ye have mutual and unfeigned love among yourselves, with peace, and if, according to the example of the holy fathers, ye shall observe this, God, the Comforter of the good, will help you, and I, abiding with Him, will intercede for you." When the bell began to toll at midnight he rose in haste, and, "running faster than the others, he enters it alone, and on bended knees falls down in prayer beside the altar." Here, a few moments later, the Brethren found him, "and," writes Adamnan, "as we have learned from some who were there present, the saint, his soul not yet departing, with open eyes upturned, looked round about on either side with wonderful cheerfulness and joy of countenance on seeing the holy angels coming to meet him."

After describing the miraculous occurrences which attended his funeral, Adamnan continues: "This great favour has also been granted to this same man of blessed memory, that although he lived in this small and remote isle of the British ocean, his name has not only become illustrious throughout the whole of our own Scotia (Ireland) and Britain, largest of the islands of the whole world, but hath reached even so far as triangular Spain, and the Gauls and Italy . . . even to the city of Rome itself which is the head of all cities."

**Conversion of the Picts.**—Soon after Columba's death, and as a result of his labours and those of his followers, the greater part of the Picts had embraced Christianity. In the extreme north, and especially in the northern islands, the heathen Scandinavians, who are afterwards referred to as Danes, gradually increased in numbers, and in 802 they pillaged and burned the monastery of Iona.

**The Angles in Scotland.**—The half-Christianized tribes of Angles who inhabited the south-east portion of

Scotland were overrun by the heathen king Penda after Edwin had been defeated and killed by him at the battle of Heathfield (633), but no heathen reaction followed.

**Conversion of the Scandinavians.**—The Irish missionaries never succeeded in converting the Scandinavians in the north, but when Christianity spread throughout Scandinavia at the end of the tenth century their conversion was gradually effected. The northmen who settled in some of the northern islands remained heathen till the close of the tenth century.

**Forcible Conversions.**—As a specimen of the forcible means by which Christianity was introduced into one of these islands a means which was all too frequently adopted on the continent of Europe, we may refer to the story told of Olaf Tryggveson, who afterwards became king of Norway. When Olaf was on his way from Dublin to Norway he put in at the island of South Ronaldsa, and, finding that the Earl Sigurd Lodvesson had only one fighting ship with him, he summoned him on board and explained to him that the time had come for his baptism, explaining to him that the alternative was his immediate execution, to be followed by the devastation of the islands. Sigurd and his followers were accordingly baptized, and he was at the same time compelled to swear allegiance to Olaf and to give his son as a hostage for his good faith.

This method of conversion, which, as we shall see, was frequently adopted elsewhere, was, as far as we know, never adopted in Great Britain or Ireland.

# VIII

## ENGLAND

**INTRODUCTION of Christianity.**—It is probable that a knowledge of the Christian faith was first introduced into Britain either by Christian soldiers or by traders who came to their shores in order to supply the wants of the Roman legions stationed in Britain. Evidence exists which shows that traders from Syria visited the north of England in very early times.* The first definite statement relating to Christians in Britain is that of Tertullian, who wrote about 208, and who speaks of " districts of Britain inaccessible to the Romans, but subdued to Christ." Origen, writing about 230, asks, " When before the coming of Christ did the land of Britain agree to the worship of the one God ? "

**St. Alban.**—The well-known story of the martyrdom of St. Alban, which, according to Bede, took place about 303, is probably founded on fact. Alban while still a pagan is said to have sheltered a Christian teacher, and having been influenced by his piety and his prayers, became a Christian in heart. Having concealed the Christian teacher from the soldiers who had come to arrest him, he was himself led before the Roman judge, and having refused to offer sacrifice to the gods he suffered death as a martyr. At the Council of Arles, which was held in the south of France in 314, three British bishops were present, who came from York, London, and Caerleon on the river Usk.† Their presence shows that by 314 a

\* See " The Conversion of Europe," p. 85 f.
† For Caerleon we ought perhaps to read Lincoln, see "Conversion of Europe," p. 91.

British Church, which probably possessed a number of bishops, had come into existence. Of the missionaries to whose labours the founding of this Church was due we know nothing. In 429 two bishops from France, Germanus of Auxerre and Lupus of Troyes, were sent over to Britain in order to counteract the teaching of Pelagius, who had propounded a doctrine of freewill which was considered to be heretical.

**The heathen Saxons.**—In 409, when the last of the Roman soldiers had been withdrawn from Britain, the Christian population had been left to defend itself as best it could against the heathen Saxons who were beginning to invade Britain. The description given by the British historian, Bede, helps us to understand how it was that the British Church well-nigh ceased to exist in England. He writes: " The impious victor . . . continued depopulating all the . . . cities and fields from the Eastern sea to the Western, with no one to oppose the conflagration, and overran almost all the surface of the perishing island. . . . Everywhere priests were slain among the altars; the prelates and the people, without any regard to rank, were destroyed by fire and sword, nor were there any to give sepulture to those who were cruelly slain. Some of the miserable remnant were caught and slaughtered in heaps upon the mountains, others, outworn by famine, came forth and surrendered themselves to the enemy for the sake of receiving supplies of sustenance, dooming themselves to undergo perpetual slavery if they were not immediately slaughtered; others in grief sought countries beyond the sea, others abiding in their own country led in fear a miserable life among the mountains, or woods, or lofty rocks, with minds always full of mistrust." If this description be a true one, it becomes easy for us to understand why it was that the missionaries by whose labours the Saxons were eventually converted came not from the British but from the Irish and Roman Churches.

**Capture of London.**—London was captured by the

Saxons about 568, whereupon Theonus the British bishop fled to Wales, accompanied by as many of his clergy as had survived. Thadioc bishop of York fled to Wales about the same time.

**Mission of St. Augustine.**—Thirty years elapsed between the departure of Theonus and the arrival of the Mission from Rome, which had for its object the conversion of the Saxons. The story of the English slave boys who attracted the attention of Gregory in the Roman market is told thus by the monk of Whitby, who was the biographer of Gregory. He writes that while Benedict was Pope there arrived at Rome certain " of our nation, with fair complexions and flaxen hair," whom, when Gregory heard of them, he expressed a desire to see. On seeing them he asked to what nation they belonged, and being told that they were Angli, he remarked " Angeli Dei " (angels of God). In reply to his inquiry, " Who is their king ? " they said " Aelli," whereupon he replied " Alleluia, laus enim Dei esse debet illic " (Alleluia, for the praise of God ought to be heard there). Lastly, he inquired to what tribe they belonged, and receiving the answer " Deire," he said, " De ira Dei confugientes ad fidem " (fleeing from the wrath of God to the faith). Gregory then asked and obtained Benedict's permission to go as a missionary to England, but, as soon as he had started on his journey, the people of Rome clamoured for his return, and messengers were sent to recall him. Bede tells the same story, but with some variations, and states that the boys were slaves. A later tradition adds that they were three in number. On the death of Benedict, Gregory was elected as bishop of Rome, and one of his first acts was to select Augustine, who was then prior of St. Andrew's monastery in Rome, and to send him as a missionary to England.

Leaving Rome in the spring of 596, he and his fellow-monks went by sea to Marseilles, and thence proceeded to Aix. Here, says Bede, " they were seized with a sluggish fear, and began to think of returning home, rather than proceed to a barbarous, fierce, and unbelieving nation, to whose very language they were strangers; and this with one consent they decided to be the safer course. They accordingly sent back Augustine to Rome that "he might by humble entreaty obtain of the holy Gregory that they should not be compelled to undertake so perilous, laborious and uncertain a journey."

Augustine was not cast in a heroic mould, and from the English point of view it was a calamity, the greatness of which it is impossible to estimate, that Gregory was prevented from carrying out his intention of becoming a missionary to the Saxons. The letter which he wrote in reply to that received from Augustine reveals his own spirit and ideals, and is worthy of a place in missionary annals. It reads : " Gregory the servant of the servants of God to the servants of our Lord. Forasmuch as it had been better not to begin good things, than when they are begun to entertain the thought of retiring from them ; it behoves you, my most beloved sons, to accomplish the good work which, by the help of the Lord, ye have undertaken. Let not, therefore, the toil of the journey, nor the tongues of evil-speaking men, deter you, but with all earnestness and zeal perform that which by God's direction ye have undertaken, knowing that great labour will be followed by the greater glory of an eternal reward. . . . May Almighty God protect you with His grace, and grant that in the heavenly country I may see the fruit of your labour; inasmuch as, though I cannot labour with you, I shall partake in the joy of the reward, because I desire to labour."

This letter, which Augustine took back to his companions, helped to revive their courage, and they started once more on their journey. They proceeded, however, so slowly that a whole year elapsed between their departure from Rome and their arrival in the Island of Thanet. The party consisted of forty members, and included interpreters whom they had obtained in France. Their interview with King Ethelbert took place in the open air, as the king feared lest, in the event of his entering a house, "if they possessed any magical powers, they might deceive and so overcome him." After hearing their message, the king replied, "Your words and promises are fair, but, as they are new and uncertain, I cannot, in order to assent to them, abandon the customs which, together with the whole English nation, I have for so long a time observed; but because ye have come hither from afar, and as I clearly perceive desire to impart to us those things which ye believe to be true and excellent, we will not molest you but give you kindly entertainment . . . nor do we forbid you to gain as many as ye can to a belief in your religion by your preaching."

In response to the invitation of the king, Augustine and his companions proceeded to Canterbury, distant about ten miles, and entered it by the road that passes St. Martin's Church, which had perhaps been built by Bishop Liudhard, who had acted as chaplain to Bertha, the Christian wife of Ethelbert. As the procession entered Canterbury, carrying a silver cross as a standard, and a picture of our Saviour "painted on a panel," the monks chanted the words, "We beseech Thee, O Lord, in all Thy compassion that Thy wrath and Thine anger may be turned away from this city and from Thy holy House, for we have sinned. Alleluia."

The teaching, and still more the prayers and self-denying lives, of the missionaries soon began to produce visible results. Thus Bede writes: "Several believed and were baptized, admiring the simplicity of their innocent life and the sweetness of their heavenly doctrine." The baptism of the king, which soon occurred, was followed by the baptism of a large number of his subjects. Augustine, having been consecrated as a bishop at Arles in the autumn of 597, returned to Canterbury, and ere long a Christian Church was established which extended as far north as London. In 602, or 603, a conference was arranged between Augustine and representatives of the British Church in Wales, in the hope that it might prove possible to form one united Church of England and Wales. The discussions which took place related to the keeping of Easter and methods of tonsure. A further object of the conference was to render possible a common effort on the part of the Britons and Saxons to evangelize the heathen, but it does not appear that this object was discussed, and the offer to join in a united missionary campaign was made conditional upon the acceptance by the Britons of Augustine's authority. When the Welsh representatives finally refused to recognize Augustine as archbishop, or to accept his demands for a change in their ecclesiastical customs, he withdrew to Canterbury. Before doing so, writes Bede, "the man of God, Augustine, is said in a threatening manner to have predicted that if they would not accept peace with their brethren they should accept war at the hands of their enemies, and if they were unwilling to preach the word of life to the English nation they should suffer vengeance of death by their hands." A bishop who could close a conference by threatening death to his opponents was not likely to prove a successful leader in a missionary campaign which should have for its object the conversion of England. In 604, says Bede, " Augustine ordained two bishops, *Mellitus* and *Justus*, to preach to the province of the East Saxons who are divided from Kent by the river Thames and border on the Eastern Sea. . . . When this province, he continues, " also received the word of truth by the preaching of Mellitus, King Ethelbert built the church of St. Paul in the city of London, where he and his successors should have their episcopal see. As for Justus, Augustine ordained him bishop in Kent at the city which the English nation named Hrofaecaestir (Rochester) from one that was formerly the chief man of it called Hrof."

Augustine died on May 26, 604. Although his name deserves to be had in honour as the head of the Mission which helped to establish a church amongst the southern Saxons, he was himself far from being an ideal missionary. He lacked both the power to initiate a missionary campaign, and the courage to carry it out, in the face of threatening dangers. A still greater defect was his lack of humility and of the power to sympathize with those who disagreed with his own opinions. This lack was painfully illustrated by his treatment of the British bishops and his failure to establish any working agreement with them. At the same time we recall with gratitude his devout and self-denying life, the remembrance of which has been a precious heritage to the English Church.

**An English Liturgy.**—One of the letters written by Pope Gregory to Augustine in reply to an inquiry as to how far it was right to form a new liturgy in order to meet the needs of a particular race, is of special interest from a missionary standpoint, as the question is one that is constantly being raised in the Mission field to-day. After saying that " Things are not to be cherished for the sake of places, but places for the sake of good things," he wrote, " From all the several churches, therefore, select the things which are pious and religious and right, and gather them as it were into a bundle and store them in the mind of the English to form a Use."

**Eadbald.**—Eadbald, who became king of Kent in 616, began by persecuting the Christians, but after a short time was himself baptized.

**The East Saxons.**—On the death of Sabert, the Christian king of the East Saxons, his three sons professed idolatry and Bishop Mellitus was compelled to leave London, and in 619 he became archbishop of Canterbury.

**The East Anglians.**—About this time the East Anglians of Norfolk and Suffolk were ruled by Redwald, who, though he had been baptized whilst on a visit to Ethelbert, resolved to combine the worship of the

Christians' God with the worship of idols, and had "in the same temple an altar to sacrifice to Christ and another small one to offer victims to devils."

His son Eorpwald, who succeeded him in 617, became a Christian, but was murdered by a pagan assassin. Three years later his half-brother Sigebert, who had been baptized in France, became king.

*Felix.*—About this time there arrived in East Anglia a missionary bishop named *Felix*, who had come to Britain from Burgundy, and had been sent by Honorius, archbishop of Canterbury, to preach in East Anglia. This "pious cultivator of the spiritual field," writes Bede, "reaped therein a large harvest of believers, delivering all that province, in accordance with the meaning of his name (Felix), from long iniquity and infelicity, and bringing it to the faith and works of righteousness and the gifts of perpetual felicity."

*Fursey.*—During the reign of Sigebert there came from Ireland a missionary named Fursey, who, "after preaching the word of God many years in Scotland (*i.e.* Ireland), could no longer bear the crowds that resorted to him, and, leaving all that he seemed to possess, departed from his native island and came with a few brothers through the Britons into the province of the English." On his arrival in East Anglia he was welcomed by the king and there, "executing his accustomed task of preaching the gospel, by the example of his virtue and the incitement of his discourse he converted many unbelievers to Christ, or confirmed those who already believed in the faith and love of Christ." On a piece of ground given to him by Sigebert at Cnobheresburg (Burgh Castle, near Lowestoft), he built a monastery. The king himself, says Bede, "became so great a lover of the heavenly kingdom that at length he abandoned the business of his kingdom which he committed to his kinsman Ecgric, and entered a monastery which he had built, and, having received the tonsure, applied himself to strive to obtain an eternal kingdom." Soon afterwards East Anglia was overrun by the heathen king Penda, whereupon Fursey retired to France.

**Northumbria.**—The story of the conversion of Northumbria, or North Humber Land, as it used to be called, is entirely distinct from that of Kent and East Anglia. The missionaries to whose labours the conversion of its people was due, came from the north instead of from the south, and their missionary methods differed in important respects from those adopted by Augustine and his companions. In 617 a Northumbrian prince named Edwin was a refugee at the court of Redwald in East Anglia, and in 625, after becoming king of Northumbria, he married his daughter. She brought with her *Paulinus*, who was consecrated as a bishop, and as a result of his teaching Edwin and a large number of his subjects were baptized. Bede writes of him : " Paulinus for the space of six years, that is till the end of the reign of that king, by his consent and favour, preached the word of God in that country. . . . So great then is said to have been the fervour of the faith and the desire for the washing of salvation among the nation of the Northumbrians that at one time, when Paulinus came with the king and queen to a royal seat called Adgefrin, he stayed there with them for thirty-six days fully occupied with the work of catechizing and baptizing, during which days from morning till night he did nothing else than instruct the people, who resorted to him from all villages and places, in the saving word of Christ, and when instructed he washed them in the water of absolution in the river Glen which was near at hand."

Edwin was defeated and killed by the heathen king Penda at the battle of Heathfield in 633, whereupon Paulinus abandoned his diocese and fled to Canterbury. Bishop Lightfoot writes of Paulinus: " The hasty and superficial work of Paulinus had come to nought. . . . The night of heathendom again closed over the land.

The first chapter in the history of Northumbrian Christianity was ended. The Roman mission, despite all the feverish energy of its chief, had proved a failure. A sponge had passed over Northumbria, and scarce a vestige of his work remained."

**Oswald.**—Oswald, having defeated his enemies at the battle of Heavenfield near Hexham in 634, established himself as king over the greater part of Northumbria. He had already been baptized whilst a refugee in Scotland, and as soon as he became king he sent to the Abbot of Iona, asking him to send a bishop to act as a missionary to his people. The first man sent, to whom Scottish tradition has given the name of *Corman*, was a man " of austere disposition, who, after preaching for a time to the English people and having effected nothing, the people being unwilling to listen to him, returned to his native country and reported in an assembly of the elders that he had not been able to benefit in any way by his teaching the nation to which he had been sent, because they were untameable and of a harsh and barbarous disposition."

**Aidan.**—One of the monks who were present when this report was made was a man named Aidan, who, according to Bede, had long been known and loved on account of his humility, his diligence in the performance of religious duties, and above all for his ability to sympathize with rich and poor, believers and unbelievers. On hearing the words of Corman, Aidan said, " It seems to me, brother, that you were more severe to your unlearned hearers than you ought to have been, and that you did not at first, in accordance with apostolic teaching, give them the milk of more easy doctrine till, having been by degrees nourished by the word of God, they might have become able to receive that which is more perfect, and practise the more sublime precepts of God."

His fellow-monks at once recognized in the speaker the man best fitted to become a missionary to the

Northumbrians, and, having secured his consecration as a bishop, they dispatched him to the court of Oswald.

The island of Lindisfarne, off the coast of Northumberland, on which he proceeded to build a monastery, became the centre of his missionary activities. As Aidan, when he started his work, knew but little English, King Oswald frequently acted as his interpreter. He was soon joined by fellow-workers who came to him from Scotland, and who were in most instances of Irish extraction. "From this time," says Bede, "many from the country of the Scots began to come daily into Britain, and with great devotion preached the word of faith to those provinces of the English over which Oswald reigned, and those (among them) who had received priest's Orders administered to those who believed the grace of baptism. Whereupon churches were built in several places: the people flocked together with joy to hear the Word, property and lands were given of the king's bounty to build monasteries, the English, great and small, were instructed by their Scottish masters in the more important subjects of study and in the observance of regular discipline, for most of those who came to preach were monks."

Aidan himself lived the life of a monk, and when he travelled on his missionary tours he went on foot. His clothing consisted of a thick woollen cape, and in winter he wore a shirt and above it a loose cloak. He had the Irish tonsure and his long hair flowed down behind. "Wherever in the course of his journeys he saw any, whether rich or poor, he would there and then invite them, if unbelievers, to embrace the mystery of the faith, or, if they were believers, he would strengthen them in the faith and would stir them up by words and actions to almsgiving and the performance of good works."

Aidan was not content with doing the work of an evangelist. He recognized the need of training Englishmen who should become the pastors and teachers of an English Church, and accordingly he gathered about him in the first instance twelve boys "to be instructed in Christ." How wisely he selected and trained his first pupils may be inferred from the fact that these included the two brothers Chad and Cedd, who became the evangelists of central and southern England, and Eata, who became abbot of Melrose, and afterwards bishop of Lindisfarne.

Oswald was killed at the battle of Maserfield in 642, but Oswin, who succeeded him, supported Aidan in his missionary labours as earnestly as Oswald had done.

**Death of Aidan.**—Aidan died on August 31, 651, at Bamborough. Referring to the circumstances of his death, Bede writes: "Aidan was in the king's country house ... at the time when death compelled him to depart from his body, after being bishop for sixteen years; for having a church and a chamber there, he was wont often to go and stay there and going thence to preach in the country round about, as he did also at other houses belonging to the king, having no personal possessions other than his church and some small fields near to it. When he was sick they set up a tent for him close to the wall at the west end of the church, and so it happened that he breathed his last leaning against a buttress that was placed on the outside of the church to strengthen the wall."

If we are justified in giving to any individual missionary the title of Apostle of England, it is Aidan to whom this title is due. Augustine's missionary labours did not extend beyond the county of Kent, and the attempts made by his fellow-monks to evangelize the East Saxons and Northumbrians ended in failure.

The West Saxons and those in East Anglia were evangelized as a result of the combined efforts of the Roman and Celtic missionaries, but the two Northumbrian kingdoms of Bernicia and Deira, and the kingdoms of Mercia and Essex, which included two-thirds of the territory occupied by the Saxon invaders, owed their conversion exclusively to the Celtic monks of which Aidan was the leader.

Of the personal character of Aidan Bishop Lightfoot writes : "I know no nobler type of the missionary spirit. His character, as it appears through the haze of antiquity, is almost absolutely faultless. Doubtless this haze may have obscured some imperfections which a clearer atmophere and a nearer view would have enabled us to detect. But we cannot have been misled as to the main lineaments of the man. Measuring him side by side with other great missionaries of those days, Augustine of Canterbury, or Wilfrid of York, or Cuthbert of his own Lindisfarne, we are struck with the singular sweetness and breadth and sympathy of his character. He had all the virtues of his Celtic race without any of its faults. A comparison with his own spiritual forefather—the eager, headstrong, irascible, affectionate, penitent, patriotic, self-devoted Columba—the most romantic and attractive of all early mediæval saints—will justify this sentiment. He was tender, sympathetic, adventurous, self-sacrificing, but he was patient, steadfast, calm, appreciative, discreet before all things."

**End of the Celtic Mission.**—Thirteen years after the death of Aidan the work of the Celtic missionaries in Northumbria was brought to an end in consequence of their unwillingness to accept the decision at which the English Church had arrived at the Whitby Conference in regard to the keeping of Easter. When Bishop *Colman* and his fellow-monks left Lindisfarne to return to Iona it became manifest how simple and frugal had been their life. "There were houses besides the church found at their departure, no more indeed than were absolutely necessary for their daily life," they had made no attempts to entertain the rich or great, "for these never came to church except to pray and to hear the word of God." Their repasts, which were of the simplest kind, were shared by their visitors even when these included the king and his courtiers. In a passage of great interest Bede describes the attitude of the people generally towards the monks, and the reception which these received when they travelled from place to place. He writes: " Wherever clergy or monks happened to come, such an one was joyfully received by all as the servant of God. And if they chanced to meet him on the way, they ran to him and, bowing their heads, were glad to be signed with his hand or blessed with his mouth. They paid great attention also to their exhortations. Moreover, on Sundays they flocked eagerly to church or to the monasteries, not to refresh the body but to hear the word of God ; and if any priest happened to come into a village the villagers quickly came together, eager to hear from him the word of life ; for the priests and clergy went to the villages for no other purpose than to preach, baptize, visit the sick, and—to put it briefly—to care for souls, and were so free from all plague of avarice that none of them received lands and possessions for building monasteries, unless forced to do so by the temporal authorities : and this custom was for some time afterwards generally observed in the churches of the Northumbrians."

**The Conversion of Wessex.**—In 634 Wessex, or the kingdom of the West Saxons, included Hampshire, Surrey, Oxfordshire, and parts of Buckinghamshire. In the previous year Pope Honorius received a visit from a man of a missionary spirit named *Birinus*, who was perhaps an Irishman, and who said that he desired " to scatter the seeds of the holy faith in those furthest inland territories of the English to which no teacher had as yet come." The Pope approved his resolve, and sent him to be consecrated as a bishop by the bishop of Milan. In the following year, Birinus landed, probably at Porchester, in Hampshire, and " finding all the people most pagan, he thought it better to preach the word there rather than to proceed further to search for others to whom he might preach." His preaching met with speedy success, and the king, Cynegils, " having been catechized, was washed in the fountain of baptism together with his people," apparently towards the end of 635. Later on Birinus established his see at Dorchester, and " having built and consecrated churches, and by his pious labour called many to the Lord, he himself migrated to the Lord (650)." The king, Cynegils, who died in 643, was succeeded by his son Kenwalch, or Coinwalch, who had " refused to embrace the mysteries of the heavenly kingdom," and was a strong upholder of heathenism. Having been defeated in battle by Penda in 645, he took refuge with Anna the king of the East Saxons. During the three years that he spent as an exile " he discerned and received the true faith." When at length he regained his kingdom, " a certain bishop called *Agilbert*, a native of Gaul, who had lived for a long time in Ireland for the sake of reading the Scriptures," came of his own accord and began to preach, whereupon the king, " observing his erudition and industry," desired him to remain as bishop. Later on the king introduced a Saxon bishop named *Wini*, and, having divided his kingdom into two dioceses, created for him an episcopal seat at Wintanchester (Winchester).

Of the later bishops of the West Saxons who were specially interested in missionary enterprises mention should be made of *Daniel*, who became bishop of Winchester in 705, and of *Aldhelm*, who became bishop of Sherborne in the same year.

**The Isle of Wight.**—In 686 Ceadwalla, having conquered the Isle of Wight, which was then " entirely given over to idolatry," invited Bishop Wilfrid to send missionaries to evangelize it. He committed this task to his nephew *Bernwin*, who was assisted by another missionary named Hiddila.

**Conversion of Mercia.**—Mercia, that is the marchland or borderland, was the name given to the territory where the West Angles marched with the Britons of North Wales and the Britons of Cumbria. Its inhabitants were Angles as distinguished from Saxons and Jutes.

Its king, Penda, was for many years the champion of heathenism, and in the course of twenty-two years killed no less than five kings, all of whom were Christians. These included Edwin and Oswald, kings of Northumbria.

**Peada.**—Missionary work was first started within the limits of Mercia by Peada, a son of Penda, who in 653 was made sub-king of the middle Angles, who occupied, roughly speaking, the present county of Leicester. Having asked for the hand of Elfleda, daughter of Oswy, king of the Northumbrian Angles, he was told that the marriage could only take place on condition that Peada became a Christian and introduced Christianity into his kingdom. Having undergone a course of instruction, and having " heard the preaching of the truth, the promise of the heavenly kingdom and the hope of resurrection and future immortality, he declared that he would willingly become a Christian, even though he should be refused the virgin." Soon afterwards " he was baptized by Bishop Finan with all his earls and soldiers, who had come with him, . . . and having received four priests who for their learning and good life were deemed fit to instruct and baptize his nation, he returned with great joy. These priests were *Cedd, Adda, Betti,* and *Diuma,* the last of whom was by nation a Scot (Irish), the others being English." These priests, continues Bede, on the return of Peada to his own people, " preached the word, and were willingly listened to, and many both of the nobles and of those of lower degree, renouncing the vileness of idolatry, were baptized daily."

By this time Penda himself had withdrawn his opposition to Christianity, and, though he was never baptized, he showed his respect for those who lived a consistent Christian life. Thus Bede writes, " He hated and despised those whom, after they had received the faith of Christ, he perceived not to perform the works of faith, and said that those were contemptible and wretched who contemned obedience to their God in whom they believed." In 655 he was killed fighting against Oswy, and the kingdom of Mercia was for a time added to Oswy's dominions. Soon after Theodore reached Canterbury in 669 Wulfhere, a son of Peada, who had become king of Mercia, applied to him for help, as Mercia was then without a bishop, and it was eventually arranged that Chad should leave York and become bishop of Mercia. By this time the conversion of Mercia was practically completed.

**Conversion of the East Saxons.**—The kingdom of the East Saxons, which included the town of London, first " received the faith " in 604 when Mellitus baptized king Sabert. On the death of the king in 616 his three sons professed idolatry and compelled Mellitus to leave London, and from 616 to 653 London and what is now the county of Essex remained heathen.

Sigebert, who became king shortly before 653, was a friend of Oswy king of Northumbria, and was by him persuaded to become a Christian. At his suggestion Oswy sent *Cedd*, a brother of Chad, and another priest to act as missionaries to the East Saxons. Bede thus describes their work : " When these two, travelling to all parts of that country, had gathered a numerous church to our Lord, Cedd returned home and came to the church of Lindisfarne to confer with Bishop Finan : who, finding how successful he had been in the work of the gospel, made him bishop of the church of the East Saxons. . . . Cedd having received the episcopal dignity . . . built churches in several places, ordaining priests and deacons to assist him in the work of faith, and the ministry of baptizing." The chief centres of his missionary labours were at Ithancestir (near Maldon), and at Tilaburg (Tilbury). Here, says Bede, " gathering a flock of servants of Christ, he taught them to observe the discipline of regular life, as far as those rude people were as yet able to receive it." Although Cedd was bishop of the East Saxons, he is never referred to as bishop of London, and it seems probable that the number of Christians there was small.

**Sighere.**—In 664, the year in which Cedd died, there were two kings of the East Saxons, Sighere and Sebbi, both of whom owed allegiance to the king of Mercia as their superior lord. Sighere apparently ruled over those who lived in or near London. Bede says that, in consequence of the ravages of the plague of which Cedd died, "Sighere, with that part of the people that was under his dominion, forsook the mysteries of the Christian faith and turned apostate. For the king himself and many of the people and of the great men, being fond of this life, and not seeking one to come, or believing that there was such, began to restore the idol temples which had been abandoned and to worship images, as if by these they might be protected against the mortality."

When news of what had happened reached Wulfhere the king of Mercia, he sent *Jaruman* the bishop of Lichfield " to correct the error and to restore the truth." His mission proved a remarkable success, and having travelled far and wide throughout the country, " he led again both the people and the king into the way of righteousness, so that, forsaking or destroying the temples and altars that they had made, they opened the churches and rejoiced to confess the name of Christ which they had opposed, desiring rather to die in Him with the faith of the resurrection than to live in the filth of apostasy among their idols." Their task having been accomplished, " the priests and teachers returned home with joy." Sebbi, the other king of the East Saxons, had not apostatized, but, " together with all his people, had devoutly preserved the faith which he had embraced."

From this time forward the profession of the Christian faith by the East Saxons continued without any further pagan reaction.

**The Conversion of Wessex.**—The last portion of England to abandon idolatry and accept the Christian faith was the district which now forms the county of Sussex. The first missionary whose work was productive of permanent results was the famous Bishop *Wilfrid* of York. Ethelwalch, king of the South Saxons had been baptized several years before the coming of Wilfrid, who arrived in 861, and he and his Christian queen Ebba did their utmost to support Wilfrid's work. The conversion of the South Saxons was facilitated by the fact that Wilfrid's knowledge of fishing enabled him to supply his converts with food during a time of grievous famine. Thus Bede writes, " The bishop, when he came into the province and witnessed the great loss caused by the famine, taught them to seek a livelihood by fishing, for the sea and their rivers abounded in fish, but the people had no skill to catch them save only eels. The bishop's men having collected eel-nets everywhere, cast them into the sea, and by the blessing of God they soon caught three hundred fishes of different kinds." These they divided into three lots, one of which was given to the poor, one to the owners of the nets, and one to the fishermen. It is probable that Wilfrid had himself learned the art of fishing when, as a boy, he had been educated at Lindisfarne.

Before Wilfrid left in order to return to the north, he built a monastery at Selsey on a site which had been given to him by king Ethelwalch, and, continues Bede, " forasmuch as the king gave him together with the possession of the place all that was there, including the lands and the men, he instructed all in the faith of Christ and washed them in the water of baptism. Among them were two hundred and fifty men and women slaves, all of whom by baptism he not only rescued from the servitude of the devil, but gave to them also bodily liberty, and set them free from the yoke of human slavery."

In 709 the first bishop of Selsey was appointed, and there were altogether twenty-two bishops of Selsey prior to the Norman conquest, after which the site of the see was moved to Chichester.

**Cornwall.**—The evidence afforded by the numerous stone crosses that have been found in Cornwall suggests that Christianity was probably introduced about the fifth century. In early times there was much intercourse between Cornwall and Brittany, and it is probable that the first missionaries to preach the gospel in Cornwall came from Brittany. Others at a later period came from Ireland and from South Wales.

**Conversion of Wales.**—There are many traditions relating to the introduction of Christianity into Wales, but they are so late and so unhistorical that it is of little use to refer to them. *Germanus*, bishop of Auxerre, to whom we have already referred, is said to have preached in Wales about 429, but the tradition relating to this is of late origin. It is probable that Christianity was spread in South Wales early in the fifth century by Picts, who had become Christians as the result of the labours of Ninian or his followers, the centre of whose labours was the monastery of Candida Casa in Wigtown Bay.

The best known of the Welsh saints is *David*, who died about 601, but the earliest life of him which we possess was not written before the close of the eleventh century, and from an historical point of view is quite untrustworthy. Of the facts relating to his life which may perhaps be true, the following are the most important. His father is said to have been the Chief of Keretica, the modern Cardiganshire. Educated in the college of Paulinus, who was a pupil of Germanus, he subsequently spent ten years in the study of the Holy Scriptures and afterwards founded, or restored, a monastery, or college, and, after residing for a time at Caerleon-on-Usk, moved to Menevia (St. Davids), of which he became bishop. It has been suggested that the choice of so remote a site was due to the fact that the tide of Saxon conquest drove the Celtic inhabitants of Wales to cultivate closer relations with their brethren in Ireland. From very early times the Welsh have worn a leek on St. David's day (March 1), in memory of the battle against the Saxons at which they wore leeks in their hats by David's advice in order to distinguish them from their enemies.

Towards the end of the seventh century many of the British Christians fled into Wales in order to escape from the oppression of the pagan Saxons. Whether or no David helped to spread the monastic system in Wales, it seems certain that the establishment of Welsh monasteries was a principal means whereby the country was eventually evangelized, but unlike the Irish monasteries these did not become centres of missionary activity beyond its own borders. We do not, in fact, possess a trustworthy record of any Welsh missionary who helped to convert any people outside Wales.

With the conversion of Wales ends our brief sketch of the missionary activities which resulted in the conversion of the British Isles.

We have omitted practically all references to the disputes relating to the keeping of Easter and other ecclesiastical questions which did much to retard the development of a united Christian Church, and have tried to lay emphasis upon the lives and work of the more prominent missionaries. At the same time we have refrained, in view of the limited space at our disposal, from recounting any of the miraculous adventures which biographers, writing many centuries after the time at which their heroes lived, have loved to tell, but which have no claim to be regarded as true. By doing so we have omitted much that would have rendered the story exciting or romantic, but those who seek to learn lessons of faith, endurance, and wisdom from the experiences of these early missionaries, which may help them to face the missionary problems that confront them to-day, cannot afford to confuse the teachings of the past by intermingling with the historical records the miraculous occurrences which devout but undiscerning biographers regarded as the proofs of a true missionary vocation.

Were it possible to recover completely the story of the past we should find that in these islands, as indeed in other lands, the people have been prepared and made willing to accept Christian ideals not by the preaching of great missionaries, but by God's "Hidden servants," who by their consistent Christian lives have commended their faith to their fellow-countrymen. We may thank God that in our islands political influence played a subordinate part as compared with that which it exerted in other countries, and that the appeal to the conscience of the individual formed a predominant note of the missionary message.

## IX

## HOLLAND

**THE peoples of Holland.**—In the seventh century when Christian missionaries first made a serious effort to evangelize Holland the northern part of the country was inhabited by the German tribes of the Frisians and Batavi, whilst the centre was inhabited by Saxons and the southern part by Salian Franks.

*Amandus*, who was appointed bishop of Maestricht in 646, established several monasteries, but his work as a missionary met with little success. In 678 Bishop *Wilfrid* of York, who was on his way from England to Rome to appeal to the Pope against Archbishop Theodore, was shipwrecked on the coast of Friesland and, as a result of his preaching which was continued throughout the whole winter, nearly all the chiefs and many thousands of their people were baptized.

**The work of Willibrord.**—In 692 Willibrord, who had been trained in Wilfrid's monastery at Ripon and afterwards for 12 years in Ireland, sailed with eleven companions for Friesland, and was welcomed by Pepin its ruler. Bede, alluding to the beginning of their work, refers to Pepin as "assisting them with his imperial authority, lest any one should offer any hindrance to their preaching, and exalting with many benefits those who were willing to receive the faith : whence it came to pass that, by the assistance of Divine grace, they in a short time converted many from idolatry to the faith of Christ."

Later on Willibrord became bishop of Utrecht. After

working in Holland for about five years he set out for Denmark where he made an unsuccessful attempt to start missionary work, but on leaving this country he brought back to Utrecht thirty boys in order that he might train them to become missionaries to their fellow-countrymen. Charles Martel, who succeeded Pepin, encouraged and assisted the missionaries and during Willibrord's later years many churches and monasteries were built throughout Friesland. Bede writes in the year 731, " Willibrord is still living, being now venerable by reason of his extreme old age . . . and after manifold conflicts of heavenly warfare sighing with his whole mind for the rewards of a heavenly recompense." He died at Epternach near Treves about 738 in his eighty-second year. St. Boniface states in a letter addressed to the Pope that Willibrord preached during fifty years to the Frisian nation. Alcuin his biographer describes him as " a devoted preacher of the word of God," but adds that a " large part of Frisian is still pagan."

We know the names of at least six other Anglo-Saxon missionaries amongst whom was " a royal prince of Northumbria," who preached in Holland at about this time.

**Wulfram.**—Wulfram, who was archbishop of Sens during the last quarter of the seventh century, is said to have made a missionary journey into Friesland, in the course of which he met with considerable success. On this occasion he baptized a son of Radbod who soon afterwards died.

Radbod himself consented to be baptized and had actually dipped one foot in the font when he stopped to ask whether, in the event of his being baptized, he might eventually hope to meet his ancestors in heaven, or whether they were in the place of torment of which he had been told. " Do not deceive thyself " was Wulfram's reply, " in the presence of God assuredly is the ordained number of His elect ; as for thy ancestors, the chiefs of Frisia, who have departed this life without baptism, it is certain that they have received the just sentence of damnation." On receiving this answer Radbod withdrew from the font, saying that he could not separate himself from his predecessors the chiefs of Frisia in order to sit down with a few beggars in the celestial kingdom.

**Gregory of Utrecht.**—The next missionary of whose work we have any detailed information is Gregory of Utrecht. Having been a pupil and disciple of Boniface he was appointed, after the death of Boniface,* as head of the church and monastery at Utrecht. Under his guidance this became a missionary college where youths from England, France, Friesland and Germany were trained with the special object of becoming missionaries to the pagan Frieslanders.

Gregory continued teaching and preaching till his seventieth year and his converts and disciples included many of noble birth amongst the Franks, the Saxons and the Frieslanders. He died in 781.

**Lebuin.**—One of Gregory's most remarkable helpers was an Englishman named Lebuin or Liafwin. On his arrival from England he built himself a hut amongst the pagans east of the river Ysell near Deventer, and his holy and austere life influenced several of the Saxon chiefs in favour of the Christian faith. Eventually, however, his oratory was burned to the ground and his converts massacred during one of the Saxon risings, whereupon Lebuin determined to make a direct appeal to the Saxons at their annual gathering for consultation and legislation which took place at Marklum in Saxony near the river Weser. We refer later to the results that followed this appeal.

He eventually returned to the neighbourhood of Deventer, and died about 775.

* For account of the death of Boniface in Frisia, see below, p. 117.

**Liudger.**—Another missionary who laboured earnestly for the conversion of his people was a Frieslander named Liudger. Born about 744 he was a pupil of Gregory at Utrecht and afterwards for three and a half years of Alcuin at York. Having been ordained deacon he returned to his own country in 773 and, on the death of Gregory in 781, he was sent to Deventer to restore the mission which had been inaugurated by Lebuin. After about seven years his labours were interrupted by the invasion of Wittekind who expelled the missionaries, burnt their churches and compelled the inhabitants of the district to become pagans. After the first conquest of the Saxons Charlemagne directed Liudger to undertake the evangelization of the people who lived in the neighbourhood of Mimegerneford (or Mimegardeford), where a missionary named Bernard had previously worked. Here Liudger built a monastery and sent out thence missionaries to preach and teach and stamp out all traces of idol-worship. In 805 he was consecrated as a missionary bishop, the site of his see being fixed at Munster. His diocese included five cantons of Friesland and the country inhabited by the East Saxons which is now part of Westphalia, extending from the river Lippe to the middle course of the river Ems. He laboured zealously as a missionary till his death in 809.

**Willehad.**—Another missionary who came from England and whose sphere of work lay in the same district was Willehad, a native of Northumbria. He was born about 730 and was a great friend of Alcuin. He began his missionary labours near Dokkum and after a while moved to the district of Groningen, the population of which was still fanatically pagan. We learn from the life of Willehad written by Anskar that as a result of his preaching and his uncompromising denunciation of their idols the people rose against him at a place called Humarcha and declared him to be deserving of death for having spoken blasphemy against their gods. Some of those present, however, withheld them from carrying out their intentions, and urged that they should delay and consider carefully before putting the missionary to death. They urged also that this form of religion was unknown to them and that they knew not whether it was offered to them by the will of the gods; that the preacher was not guilty of any crime, and should not be put to death, but lots should rather be cast in order that it might be ascertained from heaven whether he was deserving of death. This advice was accepted and, the lots that were cast having proved favourable to Willehad, he was allowed to depart in peace. He continued to labour in the neighbourhood of Drenthe with a large measure of success. Later on Charlemagne suggested to him that he should endeavour to evangelize the pagans who inhabited the district of Wigmodia, between the Weser and the Elbe, and for the next two years he worked amongst them with the result that nearly all the Saxons and Frieslanders in that district professed conversion to the faith of Christ. On the rebellion of Wittekind in 782 several missionaries were murdered and Willehad again took refuge in flight, but in 785 he returned to Friesland at the request of Charlemagne and helped to rebuild the churches which had been destroyed by the pagans. After the baptism of Wittekind missionary work made rapid progress and in 787 Charlemagne caused Willehad to be consecrated as bishop of Eastern Frisia and Saxony. After an episcopate of rather more than two years he died at Pleccatesham (Blexen) near Bremen on November 8, 789, and within three years of his death the long struggle between Charlemagne and the Saxons ended in a final victory for the emperor and in the nominal victory of Christianity.

## X

## DENMARK

**INTRODUCTION of Christianity.**—The first serious attempt to introduce Christianity into Denmark, which was made in 823, was the outcome of war. Harald Klak king of Jutland desired to make himself king of Denmark and with this object in view solicited the aid of Louis the Pious the successor of Charlemagne.

*Ebo.*—The army which Louis placed at his disposal was accompanied by Ebo the archbishop of Rheims, who hoped that he might be enabled to pave the way for a Christian Mission to Denmark. He succeeded in establishing a centre of missionary work in Holstein and three years later, when Harald Klak and his wife together with 400 followers visited Louis, they and a large part of their retinue were baptized in Mainz cathedral. When the king was about to return to Denmark archbishop Ebo suggested that he should take back with him a missionary who might confirm the king and his Christian subjects in their faith.

*Anskar.*—The missionary who was selected, and who himself expressed an eager desire to undertake this arduous task, when others to whom the work had been suggested hung back, was a monk named Anskar, or Ansgar, who was born near Corbie in the diocese of Amiens about 801. Educated first of all at the monastery of Corbie, he was afterwards transferred to New Corbie in Westphalia, where he acted as a teacher in the school and a preacher in the surrounding districts. As a boy he had frequently seen visions, in one of which he seemed to be lifted up to the Source of all light and to hear a voice saying to him " Go and return to me crowned with martyrdom." In another vision, which he had before setting out for Sweden, having obtained an assurance that his sins were forgiven, he asked, " Lord what would'st thou have me to do ? " and received the answer, " Go, preach the word of God to the tribes of the heathen." When the proposal to accompany Harald was made to him by the abbot Wala, he himself eagerly accepted, but only one of his companions, a monk named Autbert, was willing to accompany him ; and the two, after receiving encouragement and material assistance from the Emperor, proceeded together to Cologne. Here Bishop Hadebald presented him with a vessel in which to continue his journey and Harald himself joined him as a passenger. During the two years in which Anskar laboured as a missionary in Denmark he started a school at Schleswig for twelve boys whom he hoped eventually to train as missionaries. It does not appear that he achieved any large amount of success as a result of his preaching, and at the end of two years, in 828, when Harald was himself driven out of his kingdom, Anskar also retired from Schleswig, and soon afterwards went on a pioneer missionary journey to Sweden.

We refer later on to his work in Sweden. In 831 he became archbishop of Hamburg and in 849 he became also bishop of Bremen, and fixed his residence there. As soon as Anskar was established at Hamburg he began to purchase Danish, Norman and Slavonian boys, some of whom he retained with him, whilst he sent others to be educated at the monastery of Turholt between Bruges and Ypres. He hoped that amongst these boys he might find those who would become missionaries to their fellow-countrymen. His work at Hamburg was, however, rudely interrupted. The Emperor Louis died in 840, and in 845 Eric King of Jutland, at the head of an army of Northmen, sacked and burned Hamburg and destroyed all Christian churches and other buildings both in Hamburg and in the surrounding districts. A Christian library containing many books perished in the flames. Accompanied by a few clergy and scholars Anskar wandered about for some time and at length found refuge on the estate of a noble lady called Ikia at Rameshoe (Ramsola) in the district of Holstein. From this place as a centre he travelled for several years through his wasted diocese, in which the devastation wrought by the Northmen was such that the total number of churches was reduced to four.

In 854 the heathen party in Denmark defeated and killed king Horick. Horick II., who became regent over a small portion of the country, invited Anskar to send additional missionaries and a church was built at Schleswig and another at Ripen in Jutland.

As Anskar lay dying at Bremen in 865 his one regret was that his hope and expectation of winning a martyr's crown had not been fulfilled. As he was dying he repeated over and over again the words : " Lord be merciful to me a sinner : into Thy hands I commend my spirit." Rimbert, his successor and biographer, dwells upon his charity, his asceticism and his humility. He supported a hospital at Bremen for the sick and needy, he gave a tenth part of his income to the poor and gave them a share of any presents which he received, and every five years he gave an additional tithe of the animals which he possessed in order that the poor might receive their full share. Whenever he went on a tour throughout his diocese he would never sit down to dinner without ordering some poor people to be brought in to share the meal, and during Lent he would wash the feet of the poor and himself distribute bread and meat amongst them. He wore a hair shirt by day and by night ; in his earlier years he measured out his food and drink, and he chanted a fixed number of psalms when he rose in the morning and when he retired at night. He would also sing psalms as he laboured with his hands, and would chant litanies as he dressed or washed his hands, and three or four times a day he would celebrate Mass. Although his biographer attributes to him the working of miracles he never laid claim to this power himself, and when one suggested to him that he could perform miracles of healing he replied: "Were I worthy of such a favour from my God, I would ask that He would grant to me this one miracle that by His grace He would make of me a good man."

Anskar's missionary labours in Denmark were carried on under great difficulties and were frequently interrupted by the raids made by the pagan tribes who came from the north. They did not, however, succeed in obliterating his work. Thus Adam of Bremen referring to a period about fifty years after the death of Anskar, wrote, " Let it suffice us to know that up to this time all (the kings of the Danes) had been pagans, and amid so great changes of kingdoms or inroads of barbarians of the Christianity which had been planted by Saint Anskar some small part had remained, the whole had not failed."

It is interesting to compare Anskar's endeavours to make his Missions self-supporting with the policy and practice adopted in other countries.

In trying to appreciate the difficulties which the early Christian missionaries in Denmark had to face it is necessary to bear in mind the stern, unyielding character of the ancient Danes. For a Dane to acknowledge that he or his ancestors had been in the wrong was as difficult as for a Chinese to consent to loose face in the presence of his neighbours. The Dane thought it disgraceful to shed tears over his own crimes or over any calamity that might befall him, and it must have required a change which may well be called miraculous to induce him to accept the teaching of the Christian missionaries relating to the doctrines of sin, contrition and repentance.

The Danes who settled in England at, or soon after, the time of Anskar became subject to Christian influence and it is interesting to note that a Dane named Odo became Archbishop of Canterbury in 942.

*King Gorm.*—In 934 King Gorm of Denmark was compelled by the Emperor Henry to desist from the persecution of the Christians in his dominions, and to surrender to him the province of Schleswig. This province was afterwards occupied by Christian settlers who made several efforts to spread the Christian faith throughout Denmark.

**Conversion of King Harald.**—Harald succeeded Gorm in 941, and in 972 after an unsuccessful war with Otto he and the whole of his army were baptized. On this occasion the Emperor stood as godfather to his son *Sweyn.* Sweyn's conversion was, however, superficial and when he became king in 991 he re-established paganism and expelled the Christian missionaries. After his invasion of England, in the course of which he devastated wide districts and plundered churches and monasteries, he resumed the profession of the faith in which he had been baptized and took active measures to win over his Danish subjects to the same faith. Instead of applying to the Bishop of Hamburg for additional missionaries he caused Gotebald to be consecrated as a bishop in England and sent him to Denmark to act as a leader in a new missionary campaign.

*Canute.*—Canute, his son, who became an earnest supporter of the Christian cause, issued orders forbidding honours to be shown to the pagan gods and directing that his subjects should everywhere be taught to say the Lord's Prayer and the Creed and to receive the Holy Communion three times a year.

Later on Canute caused a number of bishops to be consecrated in England with a view to their undertaking missionary work in Denmark, and ere long Christianity became the nominal religion of the people of Denmark.

## XI

## AUSTRIA

**THE province of Pannonia.**—At the time when the Christian faith began to be preached in Austria and Hungary the greater part of Austria and a portion of Hungary were contained in the provinces of Pannonia and Noricum. Pannonia included the south-west of Hungary together with parts of lower Austria. Noricum included south-east Bavaria, the north-east portion of Upper Austria and the eastern portion of the Austrian Tyrol.

A Pannonian bishop named Domnus was present at the Council of Nicæa in 325 and Eusebius refers to Pannonians who were present at the dedication of the Christian Church in Jerusalem in 335. References occur to the existence of Christian communities at several other places in Pannonia early in the fourth century, but we do not know how or when these communities came into existence.

**The province of Noricum.**—Several bishops from Noricum attended the Council of Sardica, which was held about 343, and by the end of the fourth century a large part of this province had been evangelized.

The Christian communities were, however, almost obliterated by the close of the following century as a result of the invasions of the barbarians.

**Invasions by the barbarians.**—The Alemanni and Heruli attacked the north and west frontier, whilst the Goths threatened it on the east. The troops on the Danube, who had been left without pay, were unable to

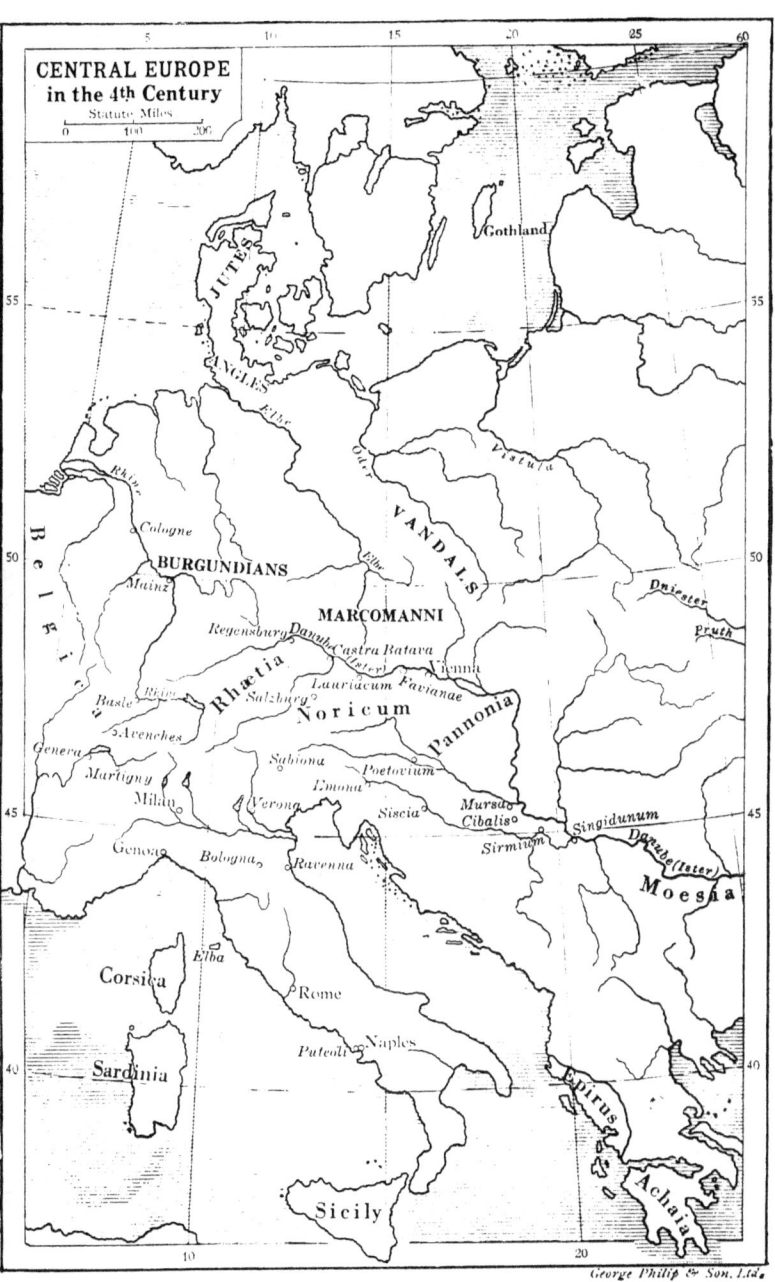

To face page 98

## AUSTRIA

offer an effective resistance, and, as the barbarians swarmed across the frontiers, the Latin-speaking population deserted their cities and, with their priests and sacred vessels, sought a refuge in Italy.

*Severinus.*—Before this happened and while the country was in a state of uncertainty and misery there appeared amongst its inhabitants a remarkable missionary named Severinus, whose biography, written by a friend and companion, has fortunately been preserved.

The uncertainty which existed in regard to his nationality and the country in which his youth had been spent, added to the romance connected with his work. When on one occasion some one ventured to say to him, " Reverend Master, from what province hath the great light come which God hath seen fit to bestow upon these lands ? " he replied jestingly, " If you suppose me to be a fugitive slave have the ransom in readiness to pay for me, if I am claimed," but, he added in a more serious vein, " What profiteth it the servant of God to name his country or race, when by keeping silence concerning them he can more easily avoid vainglory? For vainglory is like the left hand, without whose knowledge I desire through the gift of Christ to accomplish a good work, that so I may deserve to be among those on Christ's right hand and to be enrolled as a citizen of the celestial country. If thou knowest that I, though unworthy, truly desire that celestial country, what need that thou learn the earthly country of which thou askest ? But know that the God who appointed thee to the priesthood commanded me also to dwell amongst these who are threatened with many dangers."

He apparently came from some city in the East, and the language which he used on one occasion indicated that he had passed by miracle through the dangers of an immense journey.

He first appeared at Asturis, a small town a little above Vienna, and, on its destruction by the barbarians, he moved to Comagenis, where his presence served to bring hope to the inhabitants who were expecting to be attacked. The next place which he visited was Favianae, the neighbourhood of which had been plundered by the barbarians, and its inhabitants had been led away as captives. When Severinus, speaking on behalf of the people of Favianae, asked the Roman tribune Mamertinus, who was in command in the district, if he could pursue the robbers, he replied, " I have soldiers a very few, but I dare not contend with so great a host of enemies. However, if thou commandest it, venerable (father), though we lack the aid of weapons, yet we believe that through thy prayers we shall be victorious." Severinus bade him advance, confident that God would aid him, only charging him to bring back to him unharmed all whom he should capture. The attack proved successful and Severinus, having ordered the barbarian captives to be fed, sent them back to their own people in peace. It is interesting to note that this Roman tribune eventually became a Christian bishop. In the neighbourhood of Favianae Severinus built a monastery, where " he began to instruct great numbers in the sacred way of life, training the souls of hearers rather by deeds than by words."

Severinus lived a life of severe discipline and self-denial. Thus his biographer writes, " He subdued his flesh by innumerable fasts . . . he wore no shoes whatever. At midwinter, which in those regions is a time of cruel, numbing cold, he gave a remarkable proof of endurance by being always willing to walk barefoot." " He never broke his fast before sunset except on an appointed festival. In Lent he was satisfied with one meal a week, yet his countenance shone with the same cheerfulness. He wept over the faults of others as if they were his own, and helped to overcome them by such aid as he could give."

**Death of Severinus.**—Before his death, which occurred on January 8, 482, he said in the course of an address to the monks who had gathered round his bed: "Let us be humble in heart, tranquil in mind . . . knowing that meanness of garb, the name monk, the word religion, the outward form of piety, profiteth us not, if touching the observance of God's commands we be found degenerate and false." He bade all approach in succession to receive a kiss and having received the holy sacrament he commanded that they should sing a psalm. When grief kept them silent he himself started the verse, "Praise ye the Lord in His sanctuary, let everything that hath breath praise the Lord," and as he was repeating the words, "he fell asleep in the Lord."

The message which Severinus had to give to the people amongst whom he worked, apart from its missionary aspect, may be compared with that of Jeremiah. In both cases a chief part of the message consisted of a summons to repent and to give way to the invaders of the country against whom no effective or permanent resistance could be made. By the austere holiness of his life and that of his disciples he commanded the respect of the lawless chiefs and, whilst he relieved the material wants of those who had lost all that they possessed amidst the ravages and desolations of this unhappy time, he was the means of converting and adding to the Christian Church many from the ranks alike of the persecuted and the persecutors.

**Moravia.**—At the time when the Christian faith began to spread in Moravia, that is early in the ninth century, this province extended from the frontier of Bavaria to the river Drina and from the Danube to the river Styri in southern Poland. After the conquest of its people by Charlemagne some attempts were made to preach the Christian faith, but inasmuch as the missionaries who were sent were unacquainted with the Slavonic language, and conducted their services in Latin they failed to produce any lasting results.

In 863 the Moravian king *Rostislav*, or Radislav, who

was anxious to recover his independence and desired to ally himself with the Greek Empire, asked the Emperor Michael to send Christian teachers from Constantinople to instruct his people. His words, as recorded by the Russian chronicler, imply that by this date a large proportion of the people had been baptized. The message to the Greek Emperor runs: " Our land is baptized and we have no teacher to preach to us, to instruct us, and to explain to us the Holy Scriptures. We do not understand either the Greek or Latin tongue: some teach us in one way, some in another, we do not understand the meaning of the sacred Scriptures nor their import. Send us teachers who may be able to explain to us the letter and the spirit of the sacred Scriptures." On receipt of this message the Emperor called together his wise men and repeated to them the message of the Slav princes, whereupon one of them said: " There is a man at Thessalonica called Leon, who has sons well acquainted with the Slavonic language and versed in science and philosophy." The Emperor on hearing this sent to Leon and ordered him to send him his two sons, *Methodius*, and Constantine (*Cyril*), and, after interviewing them, he sent them to the Slavonic princes. The chronicler continues: " After their arrival they formed the letters of the Slavonic alphabet and translated the Acts of the Apostles and the Gospels. The Slavs rejoiced to hear of the greatness of God in their own language. . . . Then certain persons began to find fault with the books written in Slavonic and to say, ' No people ought to have its own alphabet except it be Hebrew, Greek, or Latin, as is shown by the inscription which Pilate wrote upon the cross of the Saviour.' The Pope of Rome when he heard this, blamed those who murmured against the Slavonic books and said, ' Let the words of Holy Scripture be accomplished, and let all tongues praise God.' If anyone finds fault with the Slavonic writing let him be cut off from the Church till he be corrected, for such men are wolves and not sheep."

After the work of Methodius and Cyril had continued for four and a half years a change in its political relations brought Moravia into closer touch with the Western Powers and brought the Christians in Moravia into touch with Rome. At the request of Pope Nicholas Methodius and Cyril started for Rome in 868 and his successor Adrian who had become Pope by the time they arrived declared himself satisfied with their orthodoxy and appointed Methodius as metropolitan bishop of Moravia and Pannonia. On the dethronement of the king Rostislav Methodius took refuge in Pannonia, where his use of the Slavonic Bible and liturgy aroused the dislike of the German priests, who objected to the use of any language other than Latin in the Church services. Complaints having reached Rome, Pope John VIII. wrote forbidding Methodius to celebrate Mass in Slavonic and summoning him to defend himself against the charges that had been made against him; and in 879 he arrived once more in Rome. Here, as has already been mentioned, he succeeded in obtaining the consent of the Pope to the continued use of the Slavonic language. The Pope's letter, subsequently, addressed to the Moravian king, is of special interest from a missionary standpoint. In it he wrote: "The alphabet invented by a certain philosopher Constantine (Cyril), to the end that God's praise may duly sound forth thereby, we rightly commend, and we order that in this language the messages and works of Christ our God be declared: for we are exhorted on the authority of Holy Scripture to praise the Lord, not in three languages alone, but in all tongues. . . . It stands not at all in contradiction with the faith to celebrate the mass in this Slavonic language, or to read the Holy Gospel or lessons from the Old and New Testament, properly translated and interpreted, or to rehearse any of the church hymns in the same, for the God who is the author of the three principal languages, Hebrew, Greek and Latin, created the others also for His own praise and glory. We command, however, that in all the churches of your land for the greater honour of the Gospel, it should in the first place be read in Latin, and then translated into the Slavonian language for those who do not understand Latin, as in certain churches appears to be done." Methodius returned to Moravia, but, notwithstanding the favour shown to him by the Pope, the German bishops continued to interfere greatly with his missionary labours. In 907 Moravia was invaded by pagan Magyars, or Hungarians, and when, after a war lasting for thirty years, peace was at last restored, it was united to the kingdom of Bohemia. The Slavonic language soon after this ceased to be used.

**Bohemia.**—On New Year's Day, 845, fourteen Bohemian chiefs were baptized at Ratisbon. This is the earliest item of missionary information which we possess in regard to Bohemia. There is reason to fear that their baptism indicated not so much a change of character as of politics and that their conversion was hastened by the desire of the Bohemians to secure German military aid against some of their own countrymen. A Bohemian chief named *Borzivoi* became a Christian in 871, but his subjects refused to follow his example and according to tradition he eventually abandoned his throne and lived and died disguised as a hermit. His grandson, known to singers of Christmas carols as "*Good King Wenceslas*," endeavoured to bring about the conversion of his subjects, but was murdered by his brother Boleslav who tried to restore paganism, but ended by professing Christianity himself. During the reign of his son, who succeeded him in 967, the greater part of Bohemia became Christian.

**Hungary.**—The first attempts of which we know anything to introduce Christianity into Hungary were made by the Emperor Charlemagne, who fought a series of battles (791-6) with the Huns, one of his objects being to convert them to the Christian faith. These attempts appeared to meet with success, but as soon as the soldiers were withdrawn many of the people relapsed into heathenism.

**Letters of Alcuin.**—Some letters exist which were written by Alcuin of York to Charlemagne and to Arno bishop of Salzburg in which he pleads that force should not be employed in order to make Christians. In writing to Arno, who had asked his advice in view of his proposed missionary labours amongst the Huns, he urged the need of adapting Christian teaching and discipline to the special needs of individuals and races, and insisted that the mere act of baptism could not profit unless accompanied by faith. He reminded him that the repeated lapses of the Saxons were to be accounted for by their failure to accept the faith from the heart, and urged that inasmuch as man is endowed with understanding he cannot be compelled to believe, but must be instructed and led by preaching to an acknowledgment of the truth. Special prayer, he said should be offered on behalf of missionary work, for " of what use is the tongue of a teacher if divine grace has not penetrated the heart of the hearer? . . . for that which a priest does visibly in the body by means of water, this the Holy Spirit does invisibly in the soul by means of faith." In his letters to the Emperor after the subjugation of the Huns, Alcuin says, " Now let your most wise and God-pleasing piety provide for the new people pious preachers of honest life, learned in the knowledge of the holy faith, imbued with evangelical precepts, intent also in their preaching of the word of God on the example of the holy Apostles, who were wont to minister milk—that is, gentle precepts, to their hearers who were beginners in the faith."

**The Magyars.**—At the present time nearly half the population of Hungary consists of Magyars. These are descendants of the ancient Scythians who crossed the Carpathian mountains in 889, and soon overran the whole of Hungary and Transylvania.

*Christian captives in Hungary.*—It is probable that

the Magyars gained their first knowledge of Christianity from some of the captives whom they had taken in their numerous wars, but the first Christians amongst them, of whom we have any definite record, were two princes named Bulosudes and Gylas who were baptized at Constantinople in 949. Bulosudes afterwards relapsed into heathenism, but Gylas, the ruler of Transylvania, brought back with him a missionary to help in the conversion of his people.

**Bishop Pilgrim.**—Pilgrim the bishop of Passau, who visited Hungary about 971, wrote a letter to the Pope telling of the success which missionary work had won. He stated that about five thousand of the Hungarians of noble birth of either sex " have been imbued with the catholic faith and washed with the sacred ablution." Christians also, he goes on to say, " who had been brought thither as captives from every part of the world, and who had not before been permitted to consecrate their offspring to God (in baptism) except in secret, now bring them without fear to be baptized, and all congratulate them as though they had been brought back, after a long wandering, to their own country, because they dare to build places of prayer in Christian fashion. . . . So great is the concord which exists between pagans and Christians, and so great is their mutual familiarity, that the prophecy of Isaiah appears to be fulfilled, ' The wolf and the lamb shall feed together ; the lion and the ox shall eat grass.' Thus it has come about that nearly the whole Hungarian nation is ready to receive the holy faith, and the other Slavonic provinces are prepared to believe. The harvest indeed is great but the labourers are few."

There is evidence to show that things were not nearly so bright from a missionary point of view as Bishop Pilgrim made out, but it is clear that many of the Magyars had become at least nominal Christians.

**King Stephen.**—In 997 Stephen, or St. Stephen, as he was afterwards called, became king and as a result of his efforts the Christian faith was spread throughout

Hungary and part of Wallachia. The kingdom of Hungary is frequently referred to to-day as the realm of St. Stephen. In the year 1000 he sent an embassy to the Pope to plead for his friendship and for his own recognition as king of Hungary. The Pope conferred upon him and his successors the right to call themselves "apostolic kings," and presented him with a crown which still forms part of the Hungarian crown.

The letter from the Pope is of historical interest and is worth quoting. In it he wrote: "My glorious son, all that which thou hast desired of us and of the apostolic see, the crown, the royal title, the metropolitan see at Gran and the other bishoprics, we joyfully allow and grant thee by the authority derived from Almighty God and Saint Peter and Saint Paul, together with the apostolic and our own benediction. . . . And as thy Highness did not disdain to undertake the apostolic office of proclaiming and spreading the faith of Christ, . . . we feel moved to confer besides upon thy Excellency and, out of regard for thy merits, upon thy heirs and lawful successors who may have been approved by the Apostolic See, this especial privilege: we permit, desire and request that as thou and thy successors will be crowned with the crown we sent thee the wearing of the cross may serve thee and them as an apostolic token, even as that, according to the teachings of God's mercy, thou and they may direct and order in our and our successor's place and stead the present and future churches of thy realm."

After the death of Stephen (1038) several attempts were made to restore paganism and to destroy the Christian churches but before the end of the eleventh century Christianity had become the religion of the whole population.

**The Mongols.**—The last attack by pagans was made by the Mongols, who in 1241 crossed the Carpathians and devastated the greater part of Hungary with fire and sword, the Christian churches being reduced to smouldering ruins. The desolation wrought by the Mongol raid is thus referred to by an eye-witness : "Here and there a tower half burnt and blackened by smoke, rearing its head towards the sky, like a mourning flag over a funereal monument, indicated the direction in which they were to advance. The highways were overgrown with grass, the fields white with bleaching bones, and not a living soul came out to meet them. And the deeper they penetrated into the land the more terrible became the sights they saw. When at last those who survived crept forth from their hiding-places, half of them fell victims to wild animals, starvation and pestilence. . . . The famine assumed such frightful proportions that starving people in their frenzy killed each other and it happened that men would bring to market human flesh for sale. Since the birth of Christ no country has ever been overwhelmed by such misery." *

Whilst they were still in Hungary the Mongols heard of the death of the Great Khan, whereupon they hastily retired leaving the country desolate but free.

* Quoted by Prof. Vambery in "The Story of Hungary," p. 141.

## XII

## GERMANY

**Early Christian Churches.**—Christian Churches existed in Germany early in the second century, but the spread of the Christian faith was so slow and so frequently interrupted that twelve centuries elapsed before the whole of the territory now included within the German Empire had become nominally Christian. The earliest Churches of which we have information were at Cologne and Mainz. At the latter place the majority of the inhabitants appear to have been Christians by the year 368.

**South Germany.**—At Munich and Ratisbon in Southern Germany there were Christian communities at least as early as the beginning of the fourth century. *Trudpert* an Irish hermit helped to evangelize the Black Forest (*circ.* 620) and was murdered by its inhabitants. Another Irishman named *Kilian* sailed from Ireland (in 643) with two companions, and worked as a missionary at Wurzburg in Franconia, where he was eventually murdered. By the middle of the eighth century the Alemanni, who inhabited a large part of Southern Germany and the northern half of Switzerland, had become nominally Christians, though they continued to practise many of their old heathen rites.

**The work of Boniface.**—The missionary who exerted the strongest and most enduring influence upon German Christianity and who has often been called the Apostle of Germany was the Anglo-Saxon Boniface. Before his time individual missionaries, who were for the most part

Irishmen, had acted as pioneers and had established isolated mission centres in Holland, Belgium and North Germany, but they had not proved capable of consolidating the work that had been accomplished, or of creating a united Church which might face the task of evangelizing Germany as a whole. Born at Crediton about 680, he entered, at his own request, a monastery at Exeter when only seven years of age, and later on was educated at the monastery of Nutescelle in Hampshire. Although his high birth and his intelligence would have enabled him to attain high rank in the service of the state he had set his heart upon missionary work and about 715 he sailed with three companions, to Dorstat in Frisia.

**Visit to Frisia.**—In consequence of the war that was raging between Radbod and Charles Martel he was, however, compelled to return to England, but in 718 he set out again, never to return. Travelling through France to Rome, he obtained from Pope Gregory II. a letter authorizing him to preach the Gospel in Germany or wherever he might find opportunity.

**In Thuringia.**—He first of all visited Thuringia, which roughly corresponds to modern Saxony, and endeavoured to raise the standards of life of the bishops and clergy and to reclaim those who had lapsed into idolatry. Hearing of the death of Radbod he left Thuringia, and having joined Willibrord at Utrecht, stayed with him for three years.

**In Hessia.**—Refusing Willibrord's request to become his coadjutor bishop, he started on a long missionary tour to the south-east, arriving at length in the district now called Hesse-Cassel. Here he succeeded in converting and baptizing two Hessian chiefs, who had called themselves Christians, but had at the same time worshipped idols. He was also the means of converting many other Hessians, and of establishing a monastery at Amanaburg on the river Ohm. Amongst the northern Hessians he baptized many thousands near the frontier of the Saxons—

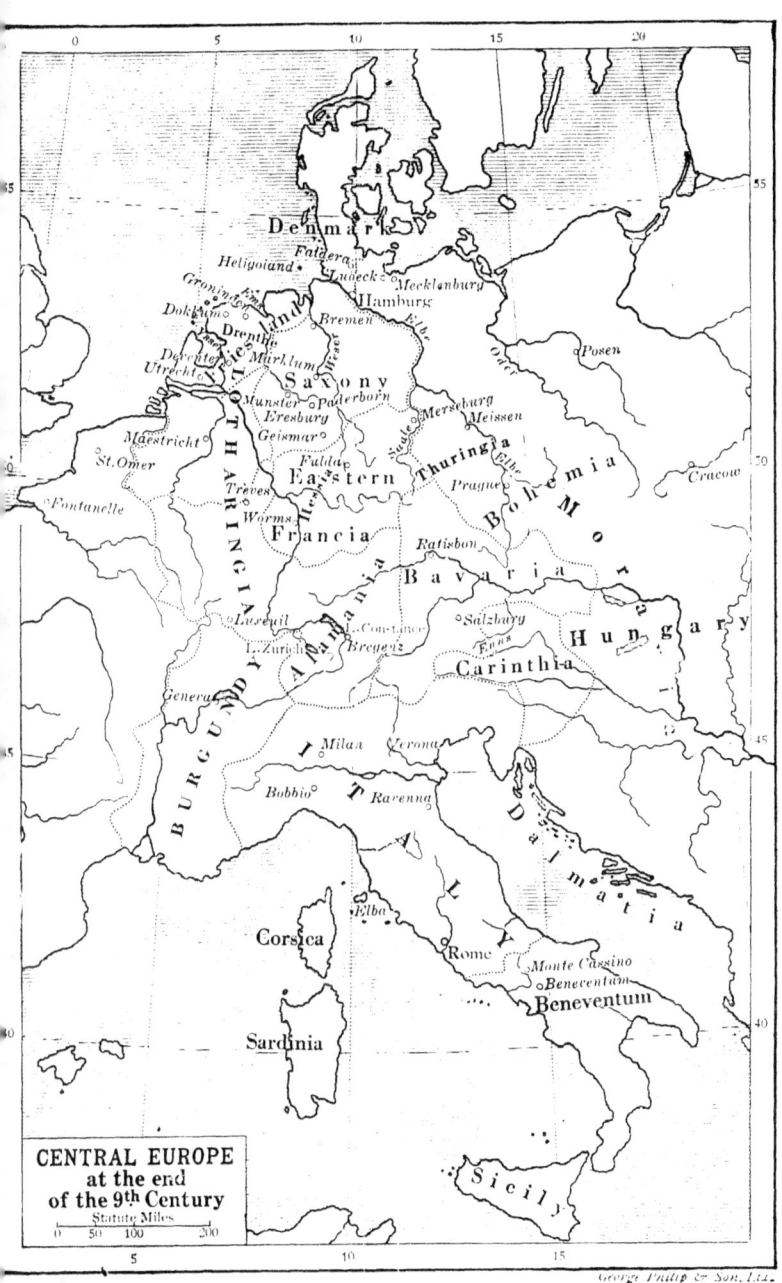

that is, near the modern Hanover, and having sent Binna (who was probably an Englishman) to report his success, he was soon afterwards summoned to Rome, and proceeded thither accompanied by a crowd of brethren and retainers. The Pope, after questioning him in regard to his missionary work, and having satisfied himself that he held the orthodox faith, consecrated him as a bishop on St. Andrew's Day, 723. Returning from Rome with a commendatory letter addressed to Charles Martel, he recommenced his work in Hessia under his protection. In the course of this letter the Pope wrote: "We have thought it necessary to send our present brother Boniface to preach to the people of the German race and to various persons dwelling to the east of the Rhine, held in the error of heathenism or up to this time fettered in the darkness of ignorance."

There is no evidence that Boniface ever invoked the aid of the secular power in order to force heathen to accept baptism, but that he was glad to avail himself of the protection and influence which political rulers were willing to afford is shown by a letter to Daniel, bishop of Winchester, in which he says, "Without the patronage of the prince of the Franks I could neither rule the people nor defend the priests or deacons, the monks or nuns; nor without his mandate and the awe which he inspires could I put a stop to the rites of the pagans and the sacrileges of idol-worship."

On his return to Hessia he found that, whilst some of his converts had remained steadfast in the faith, the majority of them, without abandoning their profession of Christianity, had begun again to offer sacrifices to trees and fountains, to consult augurs, and to practise divination. Being in doubt in regard to his method of action and the arguments which it would be best to address to the heathen Hessians, he wrote again to consult the bishop of Winchester.

**A letter from Bishop Daniel.**—His reply throws

so much light upon the methods of missionary work adopted by the more enlightened missionaries at this period that it is worth quoting at some length. In the course of his letter the Bishop wrote, " You ought not to make assertions contrary to them in respect of the genealogy of their gods, however false they be. Allow them to maintain, in accordance with their belief, that some have been generated by others . . . so that you may prove that gods and goddesses born after the manner of men are men rather than gods, and that those who were not in existence have begun to exist. . . . They should then be asked whether this world had a beginning or whether they think that it always existed and had no beginning. If it had a beginning, who created it ? . . . If they say that it always existed and had no beginning, endeavour to refute and disprove this by many documents and arguments."

After suggesting further the uselessness of sacrificing to gods when the worshippers could not even ascertain who was the most powerful amongst them, he goes on to say :—

" These and many other things . . . you ought to urge not by way of insulting or irritating them, but with large and calm moderation, and at intervals their superstitions ought to be compared with our—that is, with Christian—dogmas. Their superstitions should be referred to as a side issue, in order that the pagans may blush, being ashamed rather than exasperated, on account of their absurd beliefs."

He then advises Boniface to suggest that, inasmuch as the gods of the pagans have failed to inflict punishment upon the Christians who have overthrown their temples, they are not possessed of any real power.

**Other missionaries from England.**—Boniface's work in its early stages had been to a large extent dependent upon helpers who had come from England, and it was to England that he looked for additional helpers to

## GERMANY

enable him to secure the conversion of the heathen Saxons. Thus in a letter addressed to bishops, clergy, and abbots in England, he wrote:

"We beseech you that you will deign to remember us in your prayers. . . . Pray God and our Lord Jesus Christ, who would have all men to be saved and come to a knowledge of God, that He will vouchsafe to convert to the catholic faith the hearts of the pagan Saxons. . . . Have compassion on them, for they themselves are wont to say, 'We are of one blood and of one bone.'"

Amongst those who responded to this appeal were several women, two of whom became Heads of monastic institutions in Thuringia. In reply to a letter addressed by Pope Gregory III. to Boniface in 732 the Pope wrote:

"Great thankfulness possessed us when we read in the letter of your most holy brotherliness that by the grace of our Lord Jesus Christ you had turned very many from heathenism and error to the knowledge of the true faith. . . . You inform us that by the grace of our Lord crowds have been converted to the true faith, and that on this account you are unable to visit all and to teach them that which tends to salvation, since by the grace of Christ His faith is spread far and wide."

Six years later, *i.e.* in 738, Boniface paid another visit to Rome and remained there for nearly a year. He then desired to relinquish his work in Hessia and Thuringia, and to devote his time exclusively to work amongst the Saxons.

**In Bavaria.**—At the special request, however, of the Pope he visited Bavaria and endeavoured to reform and reorganize the work of the Church in that country. During his stay there he received a further letter from the Pope in the course of which he wrote:

"In the letters of your brotherliness you have told us of the peoples of Germany whom our God of His pity has freed from the power of the pagans, and to the number of a hundred thousand souls has deigned to gather into the bosom of Mother Church by means of your efforts and the help of Karl, prince of the Franks. We have read what you have done in the province of the Bavarians. . . . Confirm the hearts of the brethren and of all the faithful who are beginners in those western parts ; where God has opened the way of salvation, desist not from preaching. . . . Be not reluctant, most beloved brother, to undertake rough and diverse journeys, that the Christian faith may be spread far and wide by your efforts."

Pope Gregory III. and Charles Martel both died in 741, and Carloman, who became the ruler of Austrasia, Swabia, and Thuringia, sent for Boniface and encouraged him to undertake the reformation of the Church in his dominions.

*Pagan observances.*—One of the decrees issued by Carloman on the authority of a council held in the following year shows that pagan practices were still observed by many who had become nominal Christians. It reads thus :

"We have decreed that, according to the canons, each bishop in his own diocese shall take anxious care, with the help of the Count, who is the protector of the Church, that the people of God do not perform pagan rites, but entirely put away and spurn all heathen impurities. Sacrifices of the dead, soothsaying, divining, phylacteries, auguries, incantations, immolations, which foolish men carry on with pagan rites near the churches under the name of holy martyrs or confessors, provoking to anger God and His saints ; those sacrilegious fires which they call *niedfyor*, indeed all pagan observances, whatever they may be, they must diligently prohibit. . . . We have decreed also, as my father had before decreed, that whosoever performs pagan observances in any respect be mulcted in fifteen shillings."

The last clause suggests that for a rich man the sin of idolatry would not involve any very serious result.

**Boniface rebukes the Pope.**—Although Boniface professed deep respect for the authority of the Popes, he was prepared to criticize their action when it appeared to him to be deserving of blame. Thus in a letter addressed to Pope Zacharias in 742 he rebukes him for allowing the clergy in Rome to be guilty of immoralities and for permitting the growth of pagan superstition in Rome itself, the existence of which caused scandal in Germany and in other countries far distant from Rome.

**How the missionaries were supported.**—In 753 Boniface, now an old man, wrote from Mainz to Fuldrad, chaplain to Pepin, who had been crowned as king in the previous year, begging for an assurance that the band of missionary workers whom he had gathered round him would not be dispersed or suffered to want material support in the event of his own death.

His letter is of interest as showing that notwithstanding the large amount of success which had attended the labours of himself and his fellow-missionaries, their work had not been self-supporting, but had still to depend upon external assistance. " I pray our king's highness for the name of Christ the Son of God, that he would deign to inform and command me, while I still live, about my disciples what means of support he will, after (my death) provide for them. For almost all of them are foreigners. Some are priests appointed in many places to minister to the Church and peoples, some are monks in our cells, and young boys set to learn to read, and some are old and have for a long time lived with me and laboured and helped me. I am anxious about all of these, that they may not be dispersed on my death, but may receive from your highness the means of subsistence and protection, not scattered as sheep not having a shepherd, and that the people near the pagan border may not lose the law of Christ. I specially beg that my priests near the pagan border may have some poor livelihood. Bread to eat they can obtain, but clothing they cannot find there, and must obtain from elsewhere by means of those able and willing to help them to live and endure in those places for the ministry of the people, even as I in a similar way have helped them."

We gather from this letter that the number of English missionaries working under Boniface's direction was large, and that the voluntary contributions of their fellow-Christians had proved insufficient for their support. The state of things which the letter describes has had many parallels in the modern mission field. The problem was in many instances solved in early times by the establishment of endowed or self-supporting monasteries which served as centres of missionary activity.

Having received an assurance that the needs of his fellow-missionaries would be supplied after his death Boniface determined to make a further attempt to preach to the Frieslanders (in Holland) to whom he had desired to preach when he first left England.

**Final visit to Frisia.**—He clearly foresaw that this attempt would end in his own martyrdom. The account of his final visit to Frisia and of his martyrdom can best be given for the most part in the words of his biographer, Willibald. Before setting out on his voyage down the Rhine he said to Lul :

"From my longed-for journey I shall not return, for the day of my departure is already at hand, and the time of my death draws near. I shall lay down this workhouse of my body and pass to the prize of eternal retribution. . . . My son, get ready everything that you can think of for my use in this journey, and in my chest of books place the linen shroud in which my decrepit body shall be rolled." He embarked in a boat on the Rhine accompanied by three priests, three deacons, four monks, and forty-one laymen, and was joined at Utrecht by Eoban, whom he had himself placed in charge of this see. Their destination was Eastern Frisia, part of which is now covered by the Zuyder Zee. Their first efforts to evangelize this district were crowned with immediate and striking success, and a number of churches were built and thousands of men, women, and little children were baptized. After much successful work had been accomplished the missionaries, who had been scattered over a wide area, were summoned by Boniface to meet him about Whitsuntide near Dokkum, about twenty miles N.W. of Groningen, in order that the rite of confirmation might be administered to many of those who had been recently baptized.

**Martyrdom of Boniface.**—The pagan Frisians, who had become aware of the gathering, resolved to put an end at once to the missionaries and their work, and on the appointed day, which was apparently the Thursday in the second week after Whitsunday (June 5, 755), they rushed upon the Christians, who numbered fifty-two, brandishing their spears. Whilst some of the members of Boniface's party prepared to defend him, he called the clergy round him and, taking the relics of the saints which it was his custom to carry with him, he thus addressed the Christians:

"Cease, my children, from conflict, and put aside your purpose of battle, for by testimony of the Scriptures we are bidden to return not evil for evil but good for evil. For now is the long-desired day, and the voluntary time of our departure is at hand. Be strong therefore in the Lord, and suffer willingly that which He permits; set your hopes on Him, and He will deliver your souls."

To the priests and deacons and those of inferior order vowed to the service of God, speaking as with the voice of a father, he said:

"Brothers be of brave mind, and fear not those that kill the body: but cannot kill the soul that has an endless life, but rejoice in the Lord and fix on Him the anchor of your hope. He will forthwith give to you for ever your reward, and will grant to you a seat in the hall of heaven with the angelic citizens on high. . . . Receive with constancy this momentary blow of death, that ye may reign with Christ for ever."

The pagans forthwith rushed upon the little band of Christians and killed them.

**His reliance on intercessory prayer.**—As in the case of Columba a principal cause of the success which Boniface attained is to be found in the high value which he set upon intercessory prayer. His eagerness to obtain from his friends the help of their prayers for the accomplishment of his missionary work might be illustrated again and again from his letters. Thus in a letter addressed to Cuthbert, the abbot of Wearmouth, and Jarrow, dated about 735, he writes :

" With heart-felt prayers we entreat the piety of your brotherliness that we may be helped by your devout petitions who labour among the fierce and ignorant peoples of Germany and are planting the seed of the Gospel, that the fierce heat of the Babylonish furnace may be extinguished in us, and the few seeds scattered in the furrows, may spring up and multiply."

In a letter addressed to Archbishop Egbert in Northumbria he writes :

" With heart-felt prayers we entreat your clemency, that your piety would pray for us in our labours and dangers ; for great necessity presses upon us to seek the help of the just, as it is written, ' The persistent prayer of a just man availeth much.' "

It would appear from a study of Boniface's letters and the answers addressed to him that have been preserved that he did much to establish and to systematize the custom which prevailed soon after his time that bishops, heads of monasteries, and other persons should keep a list of persons both living and dead for whom they were pledged to pray at regular and frequent intervals. The " Fraternity book," or Confraternity book," belonging to a monastery contained a list of those for whom the prayers of its inmates had been promised, and frequent additions were made to its contents.

It is hard to conceive of any means by which missionary

work to-day can be more effectively strengthened and extended, or of any lesson which Boniface's life more emphatically teaches than the practice of intercessory prayer on behalf of missionaries.

**Northern Bavaria.**—An attempt was made early in the seventh century by two disciples of Columbanus to evangelize northern Bavaria and a little later Rupert bishop of Worms with twelve fellow-workers endeavoured to establish missionary work there, but with little apparent result. In 739 Boniface divided Bavaria into dioceses and did much to unify the missions that had by that time been established.

**The conversion of the Saxons.**—At the beginning of the ninth century Charlemagne's empire extended from the Baltic sea to the river Ebro in Spain, and from the English Channel far down into Italy. As a result of a long series of wars dating from 772 he had conquered the Saxons, who at this time occupied the greater part of northern Germany. Charlemagne repeatedly declared that the object of his wars was not merely to make the Saxons his subjects, but to compel them to accept the Christian faith. The Saxons at this period were a migratory people, and, apart from the fact that Christianity was for them inseparably connected with the conquest of their race, they were reluctant to accept a religion the profession of which would be followed by the building of churches that in course of time might become centres of villages or towns and would thus be the prelude of the break up of their political and social life. The fact that soldiers rather than missionaries were instrumental in the conversion of their race was one of far-reaching significance in the history of Germany.

**The work of Lebuin.**—One attempt to appeal directly to their consciences was made in or about 775 by an English missionary named Lebuin, to whose work in Holland we have already referred. He appeared at their annual gathering at Marklum near the river Weser, and arrayed in priestly garments, with an uplifted cross in one hand and a copy of the Gospels in the other hand, he presented himself to them as they were about to offer sacrifices to their national gods. Amazed at his courageous bearing they gave him at first an attentive hearing. The following are the words of his address as recorded by his biographer :

" Hearken unto me, and not so much to me, as to Him who speaks to you through me. I declare unto you the commands of Him whom all things serve and obey. Hearken, attend, and know that God is the Creator of heaven and earth, the sea and all things that are therein. He is the one, only and true God, He made us and not we ourselves, nor is there any other beside Him. The images which ye think to be gods, and which, beguiled by the devil, ye worship, are but gold, or silver, or brass, or stone, or wood. . . . God, the only good and righteous Being, whose mercy and truth remain for ever, moved with pity that ye should be thus seduced by the errors of demons, has charged me as His ambassador to beseech you to lay aside your old errors, and to turn with sincere and true faith to Him by whose goodness ye were created. In Him you and all of us live and move and have our being. If ye will truly acknowledge Him, and repent and be baptized, in the name of the Father, the Son and the Holy Ghost, and will obediently keep His commandments, then will He preserve you from all evil, and will grant unto you the blessings of peace here, and in the life to come the enjoyment of all good things. But if ye despise and reject His most salutary counsels and refuse to correct the error of your wicked heart, know that ye will suffer terrible punishment for scorning His merciful warning. Behold I declare unto you the sentence which has gone forth from His mouth and which cannot change : if ye do not obey His commands, then will sudden destruction come upon you. For the king of all the heavens hath appointed a brave, prudent and most vigorous prince who is not afar off, but close at hand. He, like a most swift torrent, will burst upon you and subdue the ferocity of your hearts, and crush your stiff-necked obstinacy. He shall invade your land with a mighty host, and ravage the whole with fire and sword, desolation and destruction. As the avenger of the wrath of that God, whom ye ever provoke, he shall slay some of you with the sword, some he shall cause to waste away in poverty and want, some he shall destroy with the misery of a perpetual captivity, and your wives and children he will scatter far and wide as slaves, and the residue of you he will reduce to a most ignominious subjection, that in you may be fulfilled what has long since been predicted, 'they were made few in number and were tormented with the tribulation and anguish of the wicked.'"

A bolder or a more unwise method of appeal, based as it was upon fear of their hated enemies, could not be conceived. We are not surprised to read that those to whom it was addressed began to pull up palings and to collect stones in order to make an end of the missionary. Happily for him an aged chief named Bruto intervened on his behalf and persuaded his fellow-countrymen to allow Lebuin to depart uninjured.

Another missionary who attempted a little later to appeal to the Saxons was *Sturmi*, a pupil of Boniface and the founder of the monastery at Fulda. He was entrusted by Charlemagne with the difficult task of appealing to the consciences of those who had been compelled to accept Christian baptism. He died, however (779), before he had seen any great results of his labours. By the beginning of the ninth century the nominal conversion of the Saxons was well-nigh complete, but, although Christianity had obtained an outward triumph, pagan beliefs and pagan practices remained for a long time intermixed with the teaching and observances of their new religion.

**Saxony.**—The present province of Saxony which formerly bore the name of Wendland, was inhabited up to the twelfth century by the Wends who were of Slavonic origin. For three centuries spasmodic efforts were made to secure their conversion to the Christian faith, but as the missionaries who worked amongst them were in most instances Germans and as the Wends and the Germans lived in a state of chronic warfare, Christianity came to be regarded as the religion of their enemies. On several occasions Christianity appeared to triumph over paganism and Christian churches began to be built throughout the country, but as soon as the standard of rebellion was raised against the Germans, a reaction in favour of paganism occurred and the missionaries were murdered or driven away. The Slavonic inhabitants of Wendland were never really converted, and it was not till the middle of the twelfth century, when the Slavonic population was practically annihilated and replaced by German immigrants, that the land could be called Christian.

*Boso*, the first bishop of Merseburg, has sometimes been called the Apostle of the Wends. He was sent by Otho I. in 936 to work amongst them, but though he learned to preach to them in their own language and succeeded in establishing three bishoprics in their midst before his death in 970, the permanent result of his work was small.

In 1047 a Slavonic chief named *Gottschalk* became a Christian and did his utmost to encourage missionary work amongst his people. He was, however, murdered by his own subjects and the chief who succeeded him was a fanatical pagan.

One of the missionaries who was put to death at this time was an Irishman, *John, bishop of Mecklenburg*, whose labours had been attended with great success. The aged bishop was cruelly beaten, and carried through the chief towns exposed to the gaze of the populace ; and finally at Rethre, after he had refused to deny his faith in order to save his life, his hands and feet were cut off and he was beheaded. His body was then flung into the street, and his head was fixed on a pole and carried in triumph to the temple of the god Radigost, where it was offered as an atonement for the contempt which had been shown to the god.

In 1125 a missionary named *Vicelin*, who had been educated at Paderborn and at Paris, endeavoured to preach to the Wends and about 1130 a number of laymen and clergy, moved by his example and influence, formed themselves into a fraternity and vowed to devote their lives to prayer and good works and to labour for the conversion of the Wends. In 1147, however, the Wends rose in rebellion against the Germans and expelled the missionaries and destroyed their churches. Vicelin eventually returned, but after his death in 1154 a further rebellion on the part of the Wends ended in a massacre which well-nigh depopulated the whole country. It was subsequently repeopled with agricultural colonists who came from the Rhine and from Holland, and who professed the Christian faith.

**Pomerania.**—The population of Pomerania from the beginning of the sixth century A.D. consisted almost entirely of Slavs. The first serious attempt to convert its peoples to Christianity was made by the Polish duke Boleslav III. who, having conquered the country in 1121, resolved to compel its inhabitants to become Christians, or, failing this, to destroy them. He ravaged the whole country with fire and sword, and murdered so many of the people that three years afterwards the survivors could point to heaps of bones which had remained unburied. Stettin, the capital, was taken, and many thousands of Pomeranian soldiers were put to death, whilst eight thousand of the people, together with their wives and children, were carried away to Poland, having first been compelled to renounce idolatry and to receive baptism.

Boleslav now attempted to find missionaries to instruct the people whom he had converted by the sword and with this object in view appealed to the Polish bishops

## HOW THE GOSPEL SPREAD

who, however, declined to attempt so forlorn a hope.

In 1122 a Spanish priest named *Bernard*, who had been consecrated as a bishop in Rome, came to Boleslav and asked to be allowed to go as a missionary to the Pomeranians. Although he knew nothing of the language or of the customs or manners of the people whom he hoped to evangelize, Boleslav, after warning him of the difficulties involved in the proposed undertaking, gave his consent. Accompanied by a chaplain and an interpreter, whom Boleslav supplied, Bernard approached the town of Julin, in the island of Wollin, barefooted and dressed as a hermit. The inhabitants of Julin, accustomed to the rich dresses of their pagan priests, regarded him with unconcealed contempt, and, in reply to his assertion that he had come as the messenger of God, they asked how it was possible to believe that the Ruler of the whole earth would send as His messenger a poor man who had not even shoes for his feet. They told him further that, if he desired to secure his safety he should return at once to the place from whence he came, and not discredit his God by pretending to be His messenger. Bernard, in reply, asked that a house should be set on fire and that he should be flung into the flames. "If," said he, "I come forth uninjured while the house is consumed, then believe that I am sent unto you by Him whom the fire and every other created thing obey." Soon afterwards, Bernard having destroyed a sacred image in Julin, the people forced him to go on board a vessel and leave them. "As you have so great a desire to preach," they said, "preach to the fishes of the sea and the birds of the air."

**The work of Otto.**—The next missionary who attempted to preach to the Pomeranians was a man who, if judged by the visible results which attended his labours was the most successful missionary in the Middle Ages. When Bernard was expelled from Julin he retired to Bamberg, the bishop of which was Otto, a Suabian of noble family who was famous for his austere life and for his successful efforts to raise the standard of Christian life amongst the clergy and laity of his diocese. Bernard related to the bishop his experiences, and besought him to make a further attempt to preach the Gospel in Pomerania. At the same time he urged him to avoid the mistake which he conceived himself to have made and to go with a large retinue of assistants and servants, dressed in costly garments and with an abundant supply of food, in the hope that those "who had scorned to accept the yoke of humility might be awed by the glory of riches and submit themselves."

Encouraged by duke Boleslav, and having obtained from the Pope the appointment of Papal legate, Otto set out in April 1124 accompanied by a body of missionaries.

**Otto at Pyritz.**—The first place visited by them was Pyritz. Arriving on the outskirts of Pyritz a little before midnight they found that a pagan festival, accompanied by revelry and drunkenness, was in progress, and they accordingly waited for daylight before announcing their errand. When the morning came the envoys of the dukes of Poland and Pomerania entered the town and explained to the inhabitants that the bishop was waiting outside and was ready to receive their adhesion to the Christian faith. Their consent having been obtained, the missionary party, with their waggons and numerous train, entered the town, whereupon Otto addressed the people, thus: "The blessing of the Lord be upon you. Blessed be ye of the Lord. We bless and thank you in the name of the Lord, because ye have refreshed our hearts by your grateful, kind, and loving reception. Doubtless ye have already heard what is the object of our coming, but it is becoming that ye should listen again and attend. For the sake of your salvation, your happiness, and your joy, we have come a long way. For ye will be safe and happy for evermore if ye be willing to acknowledge your Creator and to serve Him."

After spending seven days in giving further instruction the missionaries baptized a large number; the total number baptized during the twenty days spent by Otto at Pyritz being 7000.

**Visit to Cammin.**—Leaving behind him a certain number of clergy he proceeded to Cammin, the residence of the wife of the duke Wratislav, who was well disposed towards the Christian faith and had influenced many in favour of the new religion. He spent here nearly two months teaching and baptizing. Duke Wratislav, who arrived while Otto was still at Cammin, swore upon the sacred relics, that he would put away his twenty-four concubines and cleave to one wife. His example had a great influence upon his subjects, and many of his soldiers were also baptized and subsequently confirmed. A Christian church was then built, and one of the missionaries remained behind to serve it and to give further instruction to the converts.

**Visit to Julin.**—Leaving Cammin the missionaries proceeded to Julin in the island of Wollin. In view of the hostile feelings of the pagan population, his guides advised Otto to remain concealed on the banks of the river, and when darkness came to slip into the town unperceived and take refuge in an enclosure, which was recognized as a place of refuge, the inviolability of which would be respected by the inhabitants. In the morning, however, when their presence was discovered, the people surrounded the enclosure and threatened the missionaries with death if they did not immediately depart. Otto, who "hoped that he had been called to the crown of martyrdom," advanced with cheerful countenance, and endeavoured to speak to them, but he was knocked down and injured, and his life was only saved by the courage and strength of Paulitzky, who interposed his body between the bishop and his enemies. Beating a hasty retreat, and breaking down a bridge behind them, they reached their boats in safety. On reaching them Otto said to his companions, "Alas! we have been deprived of our expectation. The crown (of martyrdom) was in our hands, ye have snatched it away from us. May God forgive you my sons and brothers." After they had waited for five days, some of the people of Julin, several of whom were secretly Christians, visited Otto and apologized for the violence of their fellow-countrymen, whereupon Otto expounded to them the Christian faith, and at the same time threatened them with the anger of the Polish duke under whose auspices he had come, and urged them to avoid this by becoming Christians. An assembly was accordingly summoned, and, after a long discussion, it was decided that the populace would wait to see whether the inhabitants of Stettin, the oldest and noblest city in their country, would accept Christianity, and that they would then follow their example.

**Visit to Stettin.**—The missionaries accordingly proceeded to Stettin, where they attempted alternately to persuade and to frighten the people to accept the new religion. The people replied: "What have we to do with you? . . . Amongst the Christians there are thieves and robbers who (for their misdeeds) are deprived of feet and eyes, and there are all kinds of crimes and punishments. One Christian execrates another Christian. Let such a religion be far from us."

Otto, however, continued for several weeks to preach to the people at Julin and meanwhile he sent a messenger to the duke of Poland to ask his advice in view of their continued opposition to Christianity. By the time that his messenger returned he had won over a considerable number of the people and several had been baptized. In the letter which arrived from the duke he described himself as "the enemy of all pagans," and said that if the inhabitants embraced Christianity they might look for peace and a decrease of tribute, but that otherwise their land would be laid waste with fire and sword, and his relation to them would become one of "eternal enmity."

On receipt of the letter Otto proposed to the assembled people that, inasmuch as the worship of the true God could not be combined with that of idols, they should proceed to destroy the temples of the false gods. When they hung back, moved by superstitious fears, Otto and his assistants armed with hatchets and pickaxes, and having obtained their reluctant consent, proceeded to carry out the work of destruction. The first temple to be attacked was that of the Slavic god Triglav, the three-headed which contained an image of the god and was decorated with sculptures and paintings. As it had been the custom to dedicate to this god a tenth of all the spoils taken in war, its temple contained much treasure. The bishop having sprinkled the spoils with holy water and having made the sign of the Cross, distributed them amongst the people. The heads of Triglav he afterwards sent to Rome. A sacred oak, which was valued for its shade, the bishop allowed to remain, but he insisted that a horse which was used for purposes of divination should be sent out of the country and sold, and after the destruction of all heathen emblems a large number of the people were baptized. Otto's biographer refers to the change in the countenance of those who had been baptized, which soon made it easy even for the heathen to distinguish the Christians from those who had not become Christians : a change similar to that which has often been noted by missionaries in the Christian villages of South India and elsewhere. He writes : " On the faces of all who had been baptized there shone happiness and the brightness of spiritual grace, so that those who had been baptized could be distinguished from those who had not been baptized, even as light from darkness."

After a stay of five months and the erection of a Christian church in the middle of the market-place, the bishop left Stettin, and, descending the river Oder, crossed the sea to Julin, in the island of Wollin. Its inhabitants, who had previously opposed the bishop's mission now welcomed his coming and many of them were shortly afterwards baptized.

**Otto returns to Bamberg.**—Soon after this he returned to his own city of Bamberg, having first arranged for the consecration of *Adalbert*, one of his fellow-workers, as bishop of Julin. By this time Christianity had been introduced into one half of Pomerania, the number of those baptized being about 22,000, and the centres of missionary work eleven. During the next three years which Otto spent in Bamberg many of those in Pomerania who had embraced Christianity for political reasons relapsed into paganism. Moreover the missionaries whom Otto had left behind him were deficient both in wisdom and in zeal, and failed to consolidate the work which he had begun.

**Second missionary tour.**—In 1127 Otto started on a second missionary tour. Passing through Saxony he descended the river Elbe and advanced to Demmin, and later on to Usedom where he met the duke Wratislav.

*Visit to Demmin*—At a diet, or assembly, which was held here at Whitsuntide Wratislav spoke, and urged those present to abandon idolatry, and to be baptized as Christians. Presenting Otto to them, he drew their attention to the fact that although he was of noble birth and a rich man, and possessed of gold, silver, and lands, and " all that the world calls precious," he had left his life of ease and honour in order to benefit the peoples of Pomerania. He urged, too, that as his motives could not be impugned, he was deserving of an attentive hearing and of credit: they had refused to listen to the missionaries who had come to them before on the ground that they were poor: let them listen then to those who were rich. The bishop in the course of his address spoke of the divine mercy, of the forgiveness of sins, and of the gift of the Holy Spirit. His words were productive of immediate results, and some who had abandoned their profession of Christianity professed repentance, and many others, together with all the chiefs and their attendants, were baptized. Otto stayed a week in Usedom, and when he left to prosecute his missionary labours elsewhere, he adopted the plan of sending his clergy two by two into the towns and villages which he proposed himself to visit.

**Destruction of temples.**—At Wolgast he destroyed several heathen temples and arranged for the erection of a Christian church. At Gutzkow the people besought him to spare their magnificent temple, and if he wished, to convert it into a Christian church. Otto, however, feared that if this were done a reaction in favour of paganism might occur after his departure, and he accordingly insisted on its destruction. " Would you think," he said, " of sowing your grain among thorns and thistles ? No, you would first pluck up the weeds, that when the good seed is sown in your fields you may be able to obtain the crops which ye desire. So I must first utterly destroy from the midst of you this seed of idolatry and this thorn to my preaching, in order that the good seed of the Gospel may bring forth fruit in your hearts to eternal life." The objections of the people were at length overcome, and with their own hands they destroyed the temple and its idols. In its place he designed a Christian church, which by its splendour and magnificence might outshine the temple that had been destroyed. On the occasion of its consecration Otto urged Wratislav to abandon all deeds of violence and to set free all persons whom he had confined in prison in order to extract from them payment of debts. The duke's good example did much to influence his people and to show them that the new religion involved a change of conduct as well as of creed.

Otto now desired to secure the preaching of the Christian faith throughout the whole of Pomerania, but his fellow-missionaries lacked the courage of their leader, and were afraid to act as pioneers when unaccompanied by him. Even to bear him company taxed their courage to the utmost.

## GERMANY

**Stettin re-visited.**—Thus on one occasion when he announced his intention of re-visiting Stettin, where a heathen reaction had taken place, they refused to accompany him. Otto accordingly, after spending a day in solitude and prayer, resolved to proceed alone, and, taking with him his service book and sacramental chalice, he stole away in the dark. When his clergy came to call him in the morning and found that he had gone, they were struck with a sense of shame, and hurrying after him, some on foot and some on horseback, they prostrated themselves at his feet and entreated him to return with them, promising that they would accompany him on the following day. On reaching Stettin he found that the pagan priests had regained much of their lost influence, a pestilence which had broken out having been interpreted as a sign that the gods were angry at the conversion of the people to Christianity. An assault on one of the Christian churches failed of its purpose owing to the sudden illness which befell one of the ringleaders of the attack, who was a relapsed Christian. On his recovery he persuaded his fellow-townsmen to spare the church, but to erect a pagan altar by its side, so that they might secure the joint protection of the Christian and heathen deities. Soon after this, whilst the frenzy of the pagans against the Christians was still at its height, Otto and his party reached the gates of the city. On his arrival he entered one of the Christian churches, but as soon as his presence became known, armed men, led on by the pagan priests, gathered round, bent upon the immediate destruction of the church and its occupants. Otto had never been in greater danger, but his courage did not fail. After commending himself and his companions to God in prayer, he walked forth, dressed in his bishop's robes and surrounded by his clergy, who carried a cross and relics, and chanted psalms and hymns. His courage and the calmness and dignity of his action amazed and overawed the pagans, and when a lull in the tumult occurred some of those who were favourably disposed towards the Christians intervened and urged that the priests should defend their cause with arguments rather than by violence. Amongst their number was a chief named Witstack (Vitstacus), whom Otto had previously baptized, and who, after being taken prisoner in an expedition against the Danes, had obtained his release, in answer, as he believed, to prayer addressed to the Christians' God. On Sunday, two days after the attack on the church, Otto, accompanied by Witstack, went to the market-place and there addressed an assembly of the people. At the end of his address a heathen priest blew a trumpet and called upon the people to take vengeance on the enemy of their national gods. Lances were poised, and the crowd seemed about to carry their threats into execution, when once again the undaunted behaviour of the bishop overawed his enemies, and they suffered him to depart in peace. On the following day the people assembled in order to decide upon their action in the matter of religion, and, after a debate, which lasted from morning till midnight, a decision was reached that Christianity should be accepted as the true religion and all traces of idolatry should be destroyed. Otto soon afterwards received back those who had apostatized and baptized many others.

From Stettin he proceeded to Julin, where he consolidated the work that had been accomplished, and before returning to Bamberg, in 1128, he visited the other churches which he had helped to established in Pomerania. He continued to show an active interest in the Mission which he had helped to establish till his death in 1139.

**The work of Otto.**—The methods by which Christianity was spread throughout Pomerania compare favourably with those which were adopted in Saxony, and still more so with those by which, as we shall see, the conversion of Prussia was effected, and the comparison reflects great credit upon Otto. Though material force was always at his disposal he preferred to rely upon gentler influences, and never hesitated to run any personal risk in order to win the confidence and the affection of the people whom he passionately desired to help. To his faith and courage and his constant reliance upon the power of prayer more than to any political influences the results which he achieved must be attributed. He was never able to speak to the Pomeranians in their own tongue, and he does not appear to have made any arrangements for the training of Pomeranian clergy. In consequence of his failure to do this he had to introduce German clergy whose language, customs and dispositions differed widely from those of their congregations and rendered exceedingly difficult the task of establishing a Church which should be representative of the people.

**Prussia.**—If the conversion of Saxony and Pomerania makes sad reading, that of Prussia is, from a missionary standpoint, still more distressing. The word conversion cannot rightly be applied to the country, inasmuch as the majority of its inhabitants at the time when Christianity was forcibly introduced refused to accept its profession, and it was not till nearly the whole population had been massacred that it became the religion of the country, that is of the Christian immigrants by whom it was repeopled,

At the close of the tenth century, when the first attempts were made to introduce Christianity into Prussia, the population, which was for the most part of Slavonic origin, included only a small number of Germans. The country was at this time divided into eleven practically independent states, the inhabitants of which were fanatical idolators ; and in every town and village a temple was to be found. Their chief gods were Percunos, the god of thunder, Potrimpos, the god of corn and fruits, and Picullos, the god of the lower regions. Peter de Duisberg, the author of the Prussian Chronicle, writes : "They worshipped as a god every creature, whether it were the sun, the moon, the stars, or thunder, as well as birds, quadrupeds, and toads. They had also groves, plains, and sacred waters, and in these none dared to cut wood, to cultivate fields, or to fish." Every man was allowed to have three wives, who were regarded as slaves, and were expected to commit suicide on the death of their husband. On the death of the chiefs or nobles, their slaves, maid-servants, horses, hunting dogs, hawks, and armour were burnt together with the body. The description which has come down to us of the fierceness and cruelty of the inhabitants of Prussia makes it easy for us to sympathize with the difficulties which must have been encountered by the missionaries who first attempted to evangelize them.

The first of whom we have any detailed information was *Adalbert*, archbishop of Prague. After working in Bohemia for several years he visited Boleslav I., the duke of Poland, in the hope of developing missionary work in this country, but he eventually determined to go as a pioneer missionary to Prussia. Having received from the duke a vessel and thirty soldiers to act as bodyguard, he sailed to Gedania (Dantzic), on the borders of Prussia and Poland, in 997. After baptizing a number of its inhabitants he set sail again, and, having landed on the opposite coast, he sent back the vessel and his bodyguard, and, accompanied only by two priests, named Benedict and Gaudentius, disembarked on a small island at the mouth of the river Pregel. Driven away by its inhabitants, he and his companions landed on the coast of Samland on the other side of the Pregel. Having been refused a hearing by the inhabitants of this district, they began to retrace their steps, and after five or six days passed through woods, the dreariness of which they enlightened by singing spiritual songs, till at length they came to open fields. Here, after they had celebrated the Holy Communion, they lay down on the grass and presently fell into a deep sleep, from which they were aroused by a tumultuous band of heathen, who seized and bound them. "Be not troubled, my brethren," said

Adalbert, to his two companions, " we know for whose name we suffer. What is there more glorious than to give up life for our precious Jesus ? " Thereupon a heathen priest named Siggo plunged a lance into his body, and with his eyes fixed on heaven Adalbert yielded up his life. The date of his death was April 23, 997.

The next missionary to Prussia was Bruno of Querfurt a court chaplain of Otto, whom the sight of a picture of the English Boniface had led to become a missionary. Having been consecrated by the Pope as a bishop he started for Prussia in 1007 with eighteen companions, but in the following year they all suffered as martyrs. For more than a century no other attempt was made to evangelize Prussia, nor was it until two centuries had passed that any further attempt of a serious kind was made.

In 1210 a Cistercian monk named *Christian* who was a native of Freienwalde in Pomerania having obtained the approval of the Pope and with the aid of several other monks restarted the mission. In 1215 he went to Rome to report the success which he had gained and was consecrated as a bishop. At the beginning of his work in Prussia both Christian and the Pope desired to secure the conversion of the people by peaceful means, and in the hope that this might be effected the Pope addressed a letter to the dukes of Pomerania and Poland, in which he urged them not to use the spread of Christianity in Prussia as a means for oppressing the Prussians. " We beseech and exhort you," he wrote, " for the sake of Him who came to save the lost and to give His life a ransom for many, do not oppress the sons of this new plantation. but treat them with the more gentleness, as they are liable to be misled and to relapse into paganism, since the old bottles can scarcely hold the new wine."

**Order of Teutonic Knights.**—Later on when a pagan reaction occurred, which resulted in the massacre of many Christians and the destruction of their churches, a wholly different policy was adopted. Bishop Christian first founded the Order of the Knights of Dobrin and in 1219 attempted with their aid to compel the Prussians to accept baptism. When this effort proved unsuccessful he called to his assistance the Order of Teutonic Knights with which, and under the patronage of the Pope was united the "Order of the Sword." This united order undertook to subjugate the Prussians, and for nearly fifty years they carried on a remorseless war against them. Little by little they overran the country, building castles at a number of strategic points in order to maintain their conquests. Baptism was made the condition of enjoying any kind of civil rights, and those who refused to be baptized were regarded and treated as slaves. In 1233 Bishop Christian was captured by the heathen and held as a prisoner for several years until a ransom had been paid. It is true that from time to time the Pope impressed upon the knights the duty of treating the people with kindness, and upon the clergy the duty of instructing carefully those who were placed under their care, but it was not till a large proportion of the Slavonic population had been exterminated as a result of fifty years' fighting that the nominal victory of Christianity was finally secured.

With the conversion of Prussia the conversion of Germany may be said to have been completed, though another century had still to pass before the Lithuanians, some of whom live in Eastern Prussia, were nominally converted.

## XIII

# SCANDINAVIA

## NORWAY

THE first king to rule over the whole of Norway was Harald Haarfagar, who in 933 resigned his throne to his son Eric.

**King Hakon.**—Soon after the death of Harald (936) his youngest son Hakon, who had been baptized whilst residing with king Athelstan in England, succeeded in establishing himself as king.

A thirteenth-century writer, Snorro Sturleson, who is our chief authority for the early history of Norway, and who wrote in Icelandic, says: " King Hakon was a good Christian when he came to Norway, but as the whole country was heathen, with much heathenish sacrifice, and as many great people, as well as the favour of the common people, were to be conciliated, he resolved to practise his Christianity in private. But he kept Sundays, and the Friday fasts, and some token of the greatest holydays, and he made a law that the festival of Yule should begin at the same time as Christian people held it and that every man, under penalty, should brew a measure of malt into ale and therewith keep the Yule holy as long as it lasted. It was his intent as soon as he had set himself fast in the land, and had subjected the whole to his power, to introduce Christianity."

A little later the king sent to England for a bishop

and other teachers and on their arrival he proposed to his subjects that they should accept Christianity as their national religion. His proposal excited vehement opposition and at a national assembly held at Drontheim one of those present declared " We Bonders, King Hakon, . . . do not know whether thou wishest to make vassals of us again by this extraordinary proposal that we should abandon the ancient faith that our fathers and forefathers have held from the oldest times, in the times when the dead were burnt, as well as since they are laid under mounds and which, although they were braver than the people of our days, has served us as a faith to the present time." He went on to say that unless the king would abandon his proposals the Bonders would choose another king and would fight against him.

Having failed to convince his subjects by argument the king was preparing to employ force for their conversion when he was himself killed (963) whilst fighting against the sons of his brother Eric. In 977 the king of Denmark, who had conquered Norway, appointed Earl Hakon as his viceroy, having first constrained him to receive baptism. He was, however, so far from abandoning his belief in the heathen gods that on one occasion prior to engaging in a battle he sacrificed one of his sons as an offering to Thor in the hope of securing a victory.

**Olaf Tryggvason.**—Olaf Tryggvason, who became king in 995, had been baptized in the previous year by Elphege bishop of Winchester. The methods by which he spread Christianity throughout Norway can only be paralleled by those of the Moslems who first spread the faith of Islam. The chronicler Sturleson, writes, " King Olaf made it known that he recommended Christianity to all the people in his kingdom, which message was well received and approved by those who had before given him their promise, and these being the most powerful among the people assembled, the others followed their example, and all the inhabitants of the east part of Viken allowed themselves to be baptized. The king then went to the north part of Viken and invited every man to accept Christianity, and those who opposed him he punished severely, killing some, mutilating others, and driving some into banishment." To quote the words of the old Saga of Olaf: "Thereafter were all folk baptized in the eastern part of Vik and then went the king to the northern parts thereof and invited all men to receive Christianity, and those who said nay chastised he severely, slaying some and maiming some and driving away others from the land. So it came to pass that the people of the whole of that kingdom received Christianity according to the bidding of King Olaf. Wherefore in that summer and in the winter thereafter were the people of the whole of Vik made Christian."

Soon afterwards Olaf summoned the Bonders of three other districts to meet him, to whom "he offered two conditions, either to accept Christianity, or to fight." They chose the first alternative. At Nidaros near Drontheim the opposition offered by the heathen was specially strong. When the time came for the usual "sacrifice-festival" Olaf summoned the chiefs and said to them, "If I, along with you, shall turn again to making sacrifice, then will I make the greatest of sacrifices that are in use, and I will sacrifice men. But I will not select slaves or malefactors for this, but will take the greatest men only to be offered to the gods." He then named eleven principal men whom he proposed to offer as a sacrifice to the gods, the final result being that these and all the others were forthwith baptized. Before his death in 1000 he had succeeded in compelling the greater part of the inhabitants of Norway to accept baptism, but, as far as we know, he had made few efforts to instruct them in the teachings of their new religion. After his death Eric a brother-in-law of Canute ruled the country for fifteen years, during which Christianity made little progress.

**Olaf Haraldson.**—In 1015 Olaf Haraldson, who is usually known as Olaf the Saint, made himself king. He was a supporter of the new religion, but was not content with extracting a mere profession of faith from his subjects, and accordingly sent to England for bishops and other clergy to serve as instructors. Whilst, however, he preferred to make use of peaceful persuasion he did not hesitate to employ more forcible means when the former failed to produce immediate results. Thus the chronicler, referring to a progress made by the king through the southern part of his kingdom, writes, " The king proceeded southwards . . . stopping at every district and holding Things (Councils) with the Bonders, and in each Thing he ordered the Christian law to be read, together with the message of salvation thereto belonging and with which many ill customs and much heathenism were swept away at once among the common people ; . . . the people were baptized in the most places on the sea-coast, but the most of them were ignorant of Christian law. . . . The king threatened the most violent proceedings against great or small who, after the king's message would not adopt Christianity." On a later occasion, when he was visiting the people in the district of Vingulmark in the uplands, " he inquired particularly how it stood with their Christianity, and where improvement was needed, he taught them the right customs. If any there were who would not renounce heathen ways, he took the matter so zealously that he drove some out of the country, mutilated others of hands or feet, stung their eyes out, hung up some, but let none go unpunished who would not serve God. He went thus through the whole district, sparing neither great nor small. He gave them teachers and placed these as thickly in the country as he saw needful."

In no other country was the process of forcible conversion adopted more methodically, but, as the chronicler states, the king endeavoured to supplement this process by doing his utmost to encourage the work of Christian teachers, and by doing this he counteracted, to some extent, the disastrous results of his policy of compulsion. As soon as Christianity had been established as the national religion the king summoned an assembly at which a code of laws, which was apparently the joint work of himself and Bishop Grimkil, one of the bishops whom he had introduced from England, was promulgated. Special interest from a missionary standpoint attaches to the law relating to the observance by Christians of customs connected with heathenism. This law made no attempt to suppress the social customs connected with heathenism, but endeavoured to associate them with the observance of Christian customs. It directed that wherever three families could meet together and have a common feast the custom of drinking beer was to be observed, the beer having first been blessed " in honour of Christ and the Blessed Virgin for good years and peace." Fines were imposed in case of a breach of this law. A step towards the abolition of slavery was made by the law which provided that instead of offering a slave as a sacrifice at the meeting of a Thing one slave should be set free and that one should be liberated every Christmas.

So effective was the work of the Christian teachers whom Olaf introduced that Adam of Bremen, who wrote about 1070, when contrasting the condition of the people of Norway with its state in the old Viking days, could write, " After they received Christianity, being imbued with fuller knowledge, they have now learned to love peace and truth, and to be content in their poverty . . . and although they had from the beginning all been enslaved by the evil arts of wizards, now with the apostle they in simplicity confess Christ and Him crucified. . . . In many places in Norway and Sweden those who tend the flocks are men even of the most noble rank, who, after the manner of the patriarchs, live by the work of their hands. But all who dwell in Norway are altogether Christian with the exception of those who are far off beside the seas of the Arctic regions."

We should add that in the final establishment of Christianity throughout Norway the monasteries played a considerable part, though perhaps a smaller one than in most of the other countries of Europe.

## SWEDEN

A knowledge of Christianity had been introduced into Sweden early in the ninth century by Christian merchants and by slaves whom the Swedes had captured during their raids into Christian countries, but the first to attempt definite missionary work was Anskar to whose labours in Denmark we have already alluded.

Ambassadors from Sweden who came to the court of the Emperor in 829 had suggested that their countrymen would welcome Christian missionaries and it was on the invitation of the Emperor, and in response to this suggestion that *Anskar* undertook the mission. On his arrival in Sweden the king Biorn gave him permission to preach and to baptize all who desired to become Christians, and during the eighteen months which Anskar spent in Sweden a number of baptisms took place.

*Gautbert* who eventually succeeded him as a missionary to Sweden was consecrated as a bishop and laboured for about ten years, but in a rising against the Christians in 845 he was attacked and driven out of the country.

One of Anskar's first converts had been a man of rank named *Herigar* and during the seven years that followed the expulsion of Gautbert Herigar endeavoured to influence his countrymen in favour of Christianity. On one occasion when the town of Birka was attacked by Danes and Swedes under the command of Avoundus, a king of Sweden who had been expelled from his country, the inhabitants consulted their heathen priests and offered

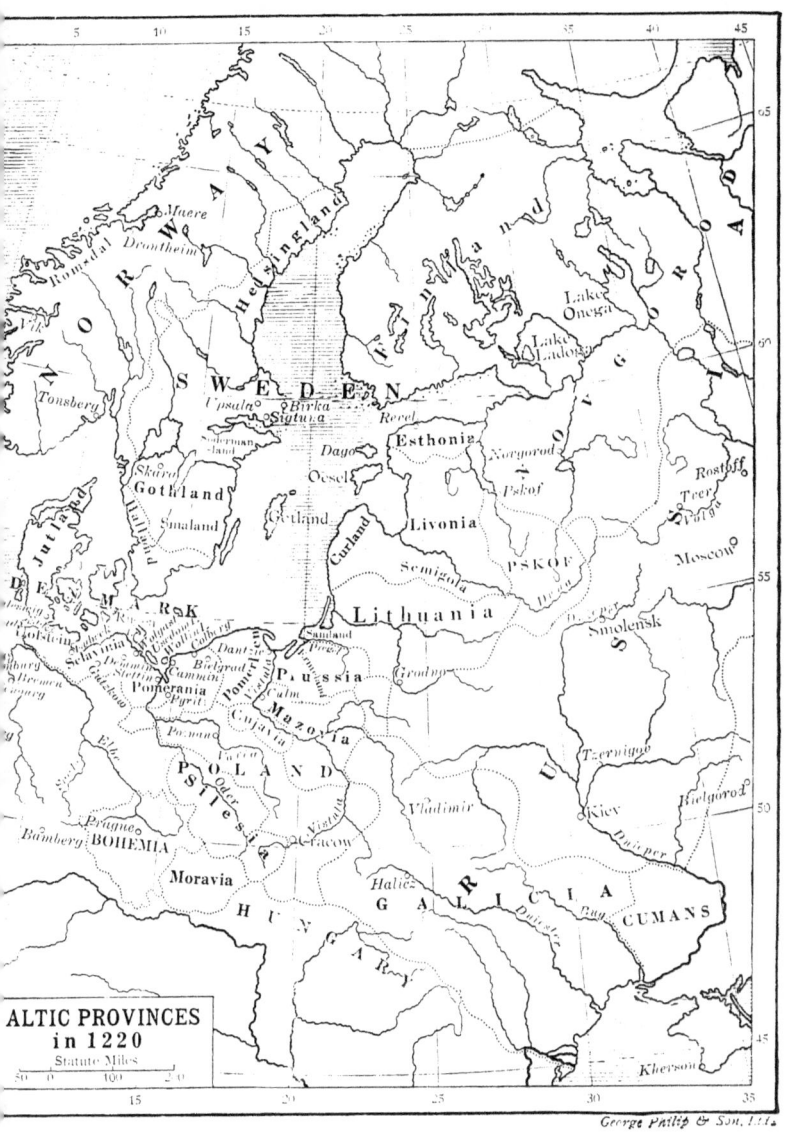

sacrifices to their gods, but failed to obtain any encouraging replies. At this crisis Herigar intervened, and, after pointing out the inability of their national gods to come to their assistance, he urged that they should make a solemn vow of obedience to the God of the Christians, and assured them that if they did so He would aid them against their enemies. The people accordingly went forth to an open plain and solemnly vowed to keep a fast to " the Lord Christ " and to give alms if He would liberate them from their enemies.

Their deliverance came about in the following way. Avoundus, who had heard that the God of the Christians was more powerful than any other god, suggested that lots should be cast in order to ascertain whether it was the will of the gods that Birka should be destroyed, and the lots proving to be unfavourable he desisted from the attack.

**King Olaf.**—In 853 Anskar revisited Sweden at a time when the feelings of the people had been excited in favour of a restoration of paganism. Nothing daunted, however, by the hostility of the people, he invited the king Olaf to declare himself in favour of Christianity. The king replied that an assembly of the people must be called and that their gods must be consulted by casting lots in order to ascertain what ought to be done. When the lots were cast the answer obtained was favourable to the request which the missionaries had made, and a proposal was accordingly made to the assembly that Christianity should be accepted as the religion of the country. While discussion was proceeding and it seemed uncertain what the vote of the assembly would be an old man stood forward and said : " Hear me O king and people : concerning the worship of this God it is already known to many of us that He can be of great help to those who hope in Him, for many of us have had experience of this in dangers at sea and in manifold straits. Why then should we spurn what is necessary and useful to us ? Once several of us, perceiving that this form of religion would profit us, travelled to Dorstede, and there embraced it uninvited. . . . Why then should we not embrace what we once felt constrained to seek in distant parts, now that it is offered at our doors ? . . . Now that we cannot secure the favour of our own gods, surely it is a good thing to enjoy the favour of this God who, always and at all times, can and will aid those that call upon Him."

Anskar returned to Hamburg in the following year and before he left Sweden resolutions in favour of accepting the Christian faith had been passed by representative assemblies in several other parts of Sweden, but, these resolutions notwithstanding, paganism continued to hold its ground for many years.

**First Christian King.**—The first Christian king of Sweden was Olof Skotkonung, usually called the Lap-king, who reigned from 993 to 1024. The king, according to Swedish tradition, was baptized by Bishop Sigfrid, who was apparently an Englishman, in 1008. Of this king Adam of Bremen writes, "Olof is said to be eminent in Sweden for a like love of religion. He in his desire to convert his subjects to Christianity, laboured with great zeal to effect the destruction of the idol temple which is in the middle of Sweden at Ubsola. The heathen, fearing his intention, are said to have passed a statute together with their king that if he wished to be a Christian he should hold as his own the best district of Sweden, wherever he desired to live, and might there establish a Church and Christianity, but should not use force to make any of the people give up the worship of the gods, and only admit such as wished of his own free will to be converted to Christ. The king, gladly accepting this statute, soon founded a church to God and a bishop's seat in West Gothland, which is close to the Danes, or Norwegians. This is the great city of Skara, for which, on the petition of the most Christian King Olof, Thurgot was first ordained by Archbishop Unwan (1013-1029). He vigorously discharged his mission among the Gentiles and by his labour, gained to Christ the two noble peoples of the Goths."

During his reign and that of his successor Christianity became firmly established throughout Sweden and though a pagan reaction occurred at Bremen in 1066, the progress of the new faith was never seriously interrupted again.

**Persuasion versus force.**—It is satisfactory to be able to record that the conversion of the Swedish people was not effected or promoted by the use of force. Stenkil, who became king in 1066, was urged by the bishops to use force in order to spread the Christian faith and eradicate idolatry, but to this request he refused to accede. His son Inge, who succeeded him in 1080, having abolished the heathen sacrifices in Svithiod, ordered all the inhabitants to be baptized, but was pelted with stones and compelled for a time to abdicate his throne.

The only other instance in which it appears that force was used was in Smaland in the twelfth century, but the forcible conversion of its inhabitants was the work of a Norwegian, not of a Swedish king.

## XIV

## RUSSIA

**Early legends.**—Legends, which have, however, no historical value, connect the name of the apostle St. Andrew with the first preaching of the Gospel in Russia. A tradition which has probably an historical foundation asserts that in 860 two princes of Kiev, named Askold and Dir, made an unsuccessful attack upon Constantinople and that they subsequently embraced the Christian faith.

*Rurik.*—The first attempt to introduce Christianity into any part of Russia appear to have been made by a Varangian prince named Rurik (d. 879) who was himself a Norseman, but of the results of his efforts we have no trustworthy information. In a treaty made between Igor a son of Rurik and the Greek emperor in 945 reference is made to the existence of a Christian church at Kiev, and the Russian chronicler states that the Russians, who had been baptized before the cross in the church of the holy Prophet Elias, swore to keep all that was contained in the treaty, whilst those who were not baptized took an oath on their swords and other weapons of war.

*Olga.*—Ten years later Olga, the widow of Igor, was baptized at Constantinople and brought back with her a priest named Gregory to act as a missionary to her countrymen, but as far as we know his labours did not meet with any great success.

**Vladimir.**—Her son Vladimir, who was the means

of spreading the Christian faith throughout Russia, and who was destined to be canonized as a saint, began his reign by murdering his brother, and by many other acts of cruelty.

During the early part of his reign he had been a strenuous supporter of paganism, and had erected near his palace at Kiev an image of Perun " with a silver head and golden beard," together with images of five other gods, to which, according to the statement of the Chronicler, the people " offered in sacrifice their sons and their daughters."

The story of his conversion to Christianity is told at length by the Chronicler and, though the account has undoubtedly been embellished, it is of considerable interest, inasmuch as it embodies the traditions that have long been accepted by the Russians.

**Story of Vladimir's Conversion.**—In 986 there arrived at the court of Vladimir envoys who represented the adherents of four different religions or forms of religion. The first to arrive, who were Bulgarian Moslems from the neighbourhood of the Volga, said to him, " Wise and prudent prince as thou art, thou hast no religion. Take our religion and render homage to Mohammed." " What is your faith ? " asked Vladimir. They replied that they believed in God and accepted Mohammed's commands to observe circumcision and to abstain from pork and wine, and they believed that after death Mohammed would give to every man the choice of a wife amongst seventy beautiful women. This last statement, says the Chronicler, attracted Vladimir, " for he loved debauchery," but the suggestions in regard to circumcision and abstinence from pork and wine displeased him. He said, " We Russians cannot live without drinking."

Next came representatives from Rome, who said, " We have been sent by the Pope, who has commanded us to say : " Your country is like our country, but your faith is not like our faith, for our faith is the light, we adore God who has made the heaven, the earth and the stars, the moon and all creatures, whilst your gods are made of wood." "What are your commandments?" asked Vladimir. They replied, "To fast according to our ability, to eat or drink always to the glory of God as our Master Paul said." "Begone," said Vladimir, "our ancestors did not accept this (commandment)."

Then came Jews who lived amongst the Khozars in the Crimea and said to Vladimir, "We have heard that Bulgarians and Christians have come to inform you of their faith. The Christians believe in Him whom we have crucified; as for us, we believe in one God, the God of Abraham, Isaac and Jacob." Vladimir asked, "What are your observances?" Their representatives replied, "Circumcision, abstinence from pork and hare, and the observance of the sabbath." "Where is your country?" he asked. They replied, "At Jerusalem." "Do you live there now?" he added. They answered, "God was angry with our fathers and has scattered us throughout the world for our sins, and our country has been given over to the Christians." He replied, "How is it that you teach others, you who have been rejected and scattered in strange lands? Do you wish that this evil should come upon us also?"

The representative of yet another form of religion appeared at the court of Vladimir, viz. a philosopher sent by Greeks, who said to him, "We have heard that Bulgarians have come to invite you to accept their faith, a faith which defiles heaven and earth; they are accursed more than any other nation, and are like to Sodom and Gomorrah." The description which the Greek proceeded to give concerning the habits of the Bulgarians caused Vladimir to spit on the ground and say, "This is an abomination." The philosopher then continued, "We have heard that men have come from Rome to teach you their faith: There is no great difference between their faith and ours." He then proceeded to explain that by withholding the wine from lay communicants the Romans had acted contrary to the directions given by Christ Himself. Vladimir said, "Jews have come and have said to me, 'The Germans and the Greeks believe in Him whom we have crucified.'" The Greek philosopher answered that what the Jews said was true and that, as a punishment for their evil conduct, God had sent the Romans to destroy their cities and to disperse them throughout the world. Vladimir asked again "Why did God descend upon earth, and did He endure such a martyrdom?" In response to this inquiry the Greek philosopher gave to Vladimir a brief *résumé* of the world's history as narrated in the Old Testament and in the Gospels, and, having explained to him the nature of the Christian faith, he went on to describe the future judgment and the pains of hell reserved for sinners. He then displayed a picture representing the separation of the just and the unjust, and the entry of the just into paradise. Vladimir sighed as he beheld the lot of those who were placed on the left hand of the judgment-seat, whereupon the Greek philosopher said to him, "If you would be on the right hand with the just, be baptized." Vladimir replied, "I will wait a little, for I desire to meditate upon all the faiths."

After taking counsel with his boyars he despatched envoys to study the various religions that had been recommended to him. The envoys who were despatched to Constantinople were deeply impressed by the service which they attended in the church of St. Sophia, and the report which they brought back put an end to Vladimir's hesitation and determined him to seek for Christian baptism. The later stages of his conversion were in keeping with his character. Before he applied to the Greeks for baptism he wished to show that, from a military standpoint, he was their superior, and he accordingly proceeded to attack Kherson in the Crimea which belonged to the Greek Emperors. Before he had completed its capture he made a vow that if he took the city he would be baptized forthwith.

**Baptism of Vladimir.**—Having effected its capture he wrote to the Emperors Basil and Constantine demanding the hand of their sister Anna in marriage, and threatening to atack Constantinople if his request were not granted. The princess, albeit with great reluctance, sailed from Kherson accompanied by a band of clergy and the baptism of Vladimir took place here. After building a church at Kherson and restoring the city to its former owners, he returned to Kiev, and on his arrival, having caused his twelve sons to be baptized he proceeded to destroy the idols which the city contained. The principal idol Perun was thrown into the Dnieper.

**Baptisms in the River Dnieper.**—He then issued a proclamation commanding his people to assemble on the banks of the river Dnieper in order that they might receive Christian baptism. His proclamation stated that " whoever on the morrow does not repair to the river to be baptized, whether rich or poor, will incur my disfavour." On the morrow there assembled an innumerable multitude of the people, together with their wives and children, and were baptized by the Greek bishops and priests who had come with Vladimir to Kiev. The Chronicler writes :

" Some were up to their necks in the water, others up to their breasts, the youngest were on the bank, men held their children, the adults were altogether in the water, and the priests stood and said the prayers, and there was joy in heaven and on earth at the sight of so many souls who were saved."

On this occasion the demon of the river was heard groaning and bewailing his expulsion from the place in which he had so long resided.

The majority of the inhabitants of Kiev suffered themselves to be baptized although Vladimir made no actual attempt to constrain them. It is to be remembered to his credit, that he himself realized the superficial character of the religious change which he had succeeded in effecting and that he adopted the best and most enlightened means for rendering the conversion of his subjects effective.

**Founding of schools.**—With this object in view he introduced, and did his best to circulate, the Slavonic translations of the Scriptures which had been made by Methodius and Cyril (see page 102), and in order that his subjects might be enabled to read the Scriptures he caused schools to be established at Kiev, Rostoff, Novgorod and many other places. Where, as was not infrequently the case, writing was regarded by the people as a form of sorcery, he went so far as to introduce a measure of compulsory education. Despite, however, the success which attended these measures, the country people generally continued to be more than half pagan in their beliefs. Before the death of Vladimir, which occurred in 1015, the greater part of his subjects had become nominally Christians, but although they had abandoned their idols they retained for centuries many of their pagan beliefs and customs. It is hard to say how far Vladimir's change of religion was due to personal conviction of the truth of Christianity and how far he was influenced by political motives, that is by the desire to become the ally and relation of the Greek emperors; but whatever may have been his real motive his title to respect is this that he was the first to render possible the spread of the knowledge of the Christian faith amongst his people.

The Chronicler tells us that *Yaroslav* one of his immediate successors transcribed, and encouraged others to transcribe, the Slavonic version of the Scriptures and built many churches and monasteries, at the same time placing clergy in the principal towns in order to instruct their inhabitants.

**Vladimir II.**—Of the Russian rulers who helped to raise the ideals of his subjects and to show them how the profession of Christianity should influence their life and conduct special mention should be made of Vladimir the Second (d. 1126), the grandson of Yaroslav and the husband of Gytha, who was a daughter of our English king Harold. We may venture to believe that he owed to his English wife part at least of the religious influence which dominated his life. The Testament which he left as a legacy to his sons helps us to understand his own character and that of some of his successors, who combined a deep respect for religion with a failure to appreciate its essential teachings. He writes :

" O my children, praise God . . . and shed tears over your sins . . . both in the church and when you lie down. Do not fail a single night to bend at least three times to the ground . . . And when you go for a ride, if you have nothing to engage your attention and know no other prayer, repeat secretly and without ceasing, ' Lord, have pity,' for this is the best of all prayers. And (to do) this is much better than to think of evil things. . . . Be not proud in your heart or thought, but say, ' We are mortal, to-day we live, to-morrow we are in the tomb.' . . . Do not hide your treasure in the ground : to do so is a great sin. . . . Avoid lying, drunkenness and debauchery, for these destroy body and soul. . . . Visit the sick, escort the dead, for we are all mortal. . . . Let not the sun find you in bed . . . as soon as you see the sun rise, praise God, and say with joy, ' Open my eyes, Lord Jesus, Who hast given me Thy beautiful light.' "

Then, without any consciousness of inconsistency, he continues :

" I have made eighty-three campaigns. . . . I have set free the chief princes of the Polovtsi . . . and a hundred others. And other princes which God has delivered alive into my power . . . I massacred them and threw them into the river Slavlia. . . . I have killed up to this time two hundred important prisoners."

**Russian Monasteries.**—The monasteries which were

founded by princes and nobles throughout Russia became centres of religious life, from which went forth many missionaries to the heathen in northern Russia.

During the two centuries which followed the time of Vladimir monks played a foremost part in spreading a knowledge of Christianity amongst the peoples of Russia and especially amongst the Finnish tribes which inhabited the greater part of Northern Russia. Settling amongst these nomad peoples, sometimes only two or three at a time, they lived at first in huts or cabins and, having won the confidence of those with whom they came in contact, and whilst endeavouring to impart Christian teaching, they taught them also how to clear the forest, to cultivate the ground, to build houses and to fish. In course of time the huts inhabited by the missionaries developed into a monastery and the settlements became towns. It was to the labours of the missionary monks that the incorporation of these Finnish tribes as an integral part of the Russian state was chiefly due.

In course of time, however, the monasteries ceased to be centres of missionary enthusiasm and, as their inmates devoted themselves more and more to a life of contemplation and asceticism, their direct influence upon the religious life of the people became less helpful.

Until the latter part of the twelfth century the Russian nation was more or less confined to the basins of the rivers Dnieper and Volga. Outside these districts Christianity made comparatively little progress and at the time of the Mongol invasion large tracts of southern Russia were still unevangelized.

**The Mongol invasion.**—At this time many of the monks who escaped being massacred by the Mongol Tartars directed their steps towards the north, and during the thirteenth and fourteenth centuries a number of missionary monasteries were founded in the northern districts, more particularly amongst the Finnish tribes which bordered on Russia.

## 154  HOW THE GOSPEL SPREAD

By the beginning of the thirteenth century, when the Tartar Mongols, who were to dominate Russia for two centuries, first began their invasions, the greater part of Russia had become nominally Christian. The great battle which was fought at Kalka in 1224 checked their invasion for the moment, but twelve years later they returned and overran the greater part of the country, razing the chief towns, including Kiev, and destroying the Christian churches. How ruthlessly the Mongols massacred the inhabitants of the countries which they conquered may be gathered from the statement of Howorth in his history of the Mongols that between the years 1211 and 1223, " 18,470,000 beings perished in China and Tangut alone at the hands of Jengis and his followers."

Up to 1313 when Usbek Khan embraced Islam the Tartar Mongols had been pagans, but from this date they became the supporters of the religion of Mohammed.

**Sergius**, whose name is known and revered throughout Russia, was born at Rostoff in 1315 and whilst still a young man he went to live, first of all with his brother, and afterwards alone amongst the wild beasts in the thick forest about forty-three miles north-east of Moscow. His holy life soon attracted to him disciples, and with their aid he built a little wooden church dedicated to the Holy Trinity (Troitskaia). The monastery which arose on the same site became the largest and most influential in Russia and from it went forth thousands of monks and ascetics to labour both in the central and southern parts of Russia and amongst the tribes of the north.

Other monasteries, the monks from which contributed towards the evangelization of some of the outlying parts of the Russian Empire in the thirteenth and fourteenth centuries, are the monastery of the Assumption on the shores of Lake Onega, founded for the prosecution of missionary work amongst the Lopars (Laplanders) : one on an island in the Kubansky Lake, the monks of which strove to evangelize the savage tribes of Tehudes (Finns) : the Solovetsky monastery on an island in the White Sea, the monks of which laboured amongst the inhabitants along the coast, and one on Lake Ladoga which was a centre of missionary work amongst the Carelians.

*Stephen.*—During the latter half of the fourteenth century a missionary named Stephen, succeeded in winning to the Christian faith the Ziranes who inhabited the district of Great Perm in the south-east of Russia. In 1378 he built a church on the river Viuma which served as a centre of his missionary work. The language of the Ziranes which he had known from his boyhood was reduced by him to writing after he had himself composed an alphabet for the purpose. He then translated parts of the Bible and of the liturgy into the Zirane language, and the Services in his church were conducted by him in the language of the people. After his consecration as a bishop in 1383 he established many churches and schools throughout the province of Perm, and ordained some of the students who had been educated in his schools as priests. He died at Moscow in 1401.

**Livonia.**—The Lieflanders who inhabited Livonia, one of the Baltic provinces of Russia, after resisting successfully the efforts made by Danish kings to introduce Christianity by force of arms, allowed a monk named *Meinhard* to build a church at Ukskull near Riga. In 1186 he was consecrated as a bishop and laboured as a missionary, though with little visible success, till his death in 1196. His successor, Berthold, anxious to obtain more speedy results collected an armed force with the help of Pope Innocent III. and fought a battle with the Lieflanders in which he was himself killed.

The next bishop, *Albert of Bremen*, who sailed up the river Duna in 1200 with a fleet and accompanied by a large armed force reduced the Lieflanders to subjection and founded the town of Riga in 1201, to which place the bishopric of Ukskull was transferred. His efforts, however, to evangelize the people met with scant success, and in the following year, with the approval of the Pope, he invoked the aid of the Knights of the "Order of the Sword" in order to promote the forcible conversion of the Lieflanders. Ruthless war was waged by the knights, and peace was granted to each separate district only on condition that its inhabitants should be baptized.

One missionary, a monk named *Sigfrid*, who was in charge of the church at Holm, adopted a different method of evangelization and his earnestness and piety induced many to seek for Christian instruction and baptism.

By 1229, the year in which Bishop Albert died, the opposition of the Lieflanders had been completely broken down and the majority of them had been baptized.

**Esthonia.**—Esthonia, another of the Baltic provinces, was invaded by the Danes in the eleventh century. After forcibly baptizing a few of its inhabitants they were repulsed and Esthonia remained heathen till 1219, when the Danish king Valdemar II, conquered the province and compelled its inhabitants to accept the Christian faith. In 1347 Esthonia was sold by the Danes to the Knights of the "Order of the Sword."

**Lithuania.**—In 1250 Mendowg, the ruler of Lithuania, having been defeated by the Livonian Knights agreed to accept baptism, but in 1260, on regaining his independence, he relapsed into heathenism. In 1345 Olgerd, the ruler of Lithuania married a Christian wife, and was himself baptized. He continued, however, to offer sacrifices to the national gods. His son, Yagello in 1386 married the Polish Queen Yadviga, who was a Christian, and agreed to introduce Christianity into Lithuania. Up to this time the Lithuanians had worshipped the stars and the god of thunder and had specially venerated serpents and lizards. Adam of Bremen writes of them,

" They venerate serpents and birds to whom they even offer living men bought from the merchants, after they have been carefully examined to see that they have no spot on their bodies." In the fourteenth century their chief priest Krive-Kriveyto (judge of judges) superintended seventeen classes of priests and elders who worshipped in the forests, and long after the introduction of Christianity veneration was paid to oak trees both by the Lithuanians and the Letts. These also maintained a perpetual fire, the priests in charge of which were specially consulted by the friends of those who were sick.

Polish clergy were introduced by Yagello and, moved by his example, and his exhortations, large numbers of his people were baptized.

**Finland.**—In 1157 Erik king of Sweden, established himself on the south-western coast of Finland. Henrick, bishop of Upsala, who accompanied Erik, preached the gospel to the Finns and suffered a martyr's death about 1178, but within the next fifty years missionary work made considerable progress and an independent Church of Finland was established.

**Work amongst the Tartars.**—Although the great majority of the inhabitants of European Russia had accepted Christianity by the end of the thirteenth century, there remained great numbers of Tartars and others in the south and south-east who continued as pagans.

Missionary work was carried on with a considerable amount of success by St. Juri (Gurius), the first bishop of Kazan (1555-64), which lies about halfway between Moscow and the Ural mountains. As a result of his labours and those of Bishop Germanus, Christian communities were established in the towns, but many inhabitants of the villages are still either pagans or Mohammedans.

During the seventeenth and eighteenth centuries a hundred thousand Tartars were forced by the Russian government to accept baptism but their descendants are Christian only in name and many have openly embraced Islam.

In 1847 *Nicholai Ilminsky* undertook the task of translating the Bible and Service books into a language which the Tartars could understand, and having established a missionary school at Kazan sent out the scholars whom he had trained, who established other schools and helped to evangelize many districts in the same neighbourhood. The Kazan Translation Committee has published translations in twenty different languages which are spoken either in European Russia or Siberia.

Prior to the war the Russian Empire contained twenty million Moslems of whom three and a half million were in European Russia.

## XV

## A GENERAL SURVEY

IN accordance with the scheme adopted throughout this book we have tried to follow the progress of missionary work as it developed in the separate countries of Europe. One drawback attaching to this method is that it is difficult for the reader to appreciate the progress that had been attained in Europe as a whole at any given time. In order to render it easier to do this we have inserted the chronological table which appears on the following pages.

From this it will be seen that the labours of the missionaries in Western Europe, that is in Great Britain, France, Belgium, and Spain, were nearly completed before any serious attempt had been made to evangelize Scandinavia, or the greater part of Central and Eastern Europe.

## CHRISTIAN MISSIONS IN WESTERN EUROPE.

| BRITISH ISLES. | FRANCE AND SPAIN. |
|---|---|
| | St. Paul in Spain . . 66 ? |
| | Persecutions at Lyons and Vienne . . . . 177 |
| | Spanish martyrs in persecutions of Valerian . 256–260 |
| Martyrdom of St. Alban . 303 | Spanish martyrs in persecutions of Diocletian . 303–4 |
| Three British bpp. at Council of Arles . . . . 314 | Council of Elvira in Spain . 306 |
| | Hilary, bp. of Poitiers . . 350 |
| | Martin of Tours . . 316–97 |
| | Goths invade Spain . . 414 |
| | Germanus, bp. of Auxerre 418–49 |
| Patrick consecrated as bishop 432 | Conversion of East Burgundians . . . . 430 |
| Ninian in Scotland, d. . 432 | |
| | Eleutherius, bp. of Tournai . 487 |
| Columbia settles in Iona . 563 | Conversion of Clovis . . 496 |
| | Columbanus . . 573–610 |
| Augustine at Canterbury 597–604 | |
| David, bp. of Menevia in Wales . . . 601 ? | |
| Kentigern (St. Mungo), d. . 603 | |
| Paulinus in Northumbria 625–33 | Livinus, Apostle of Brabant . 633 |
| Wessex, Conversion of . 634 | |
| Aidan at Lindisfarne . 635–51 | Eligius missionary to the Frisians . . . . 641 |
| Mercia, Cedd in . . . 653 | |
| East Saxons, Baptism of Sigebert king of . . 653 | |
| Whitby, Council of . . 664 | |
| London, Bp. Jaruman in . 665 | |
| | Frisia, Wilfrid in . . 678 |
| Sussex, Wilfrid in . . 681 | Frisia, Willibrord in . 692–738 |
| | Arrival of Moors in Spain . 710 |
| | Boniface, death of, in Frisia 755 |
| | Liudger, in Frisia, d. . . 809 |

## A GENERAL SURVEY

### CONVERSION OF SCANDINAVIA AND EASTERN EUROPE.

**DENMARK AND SCANDINAVIA.**

**CENTRAL AND EASTERN EUROPE.**

| | |
|---|---|
| Ulfilas Apostle to the Goths, d. | 381 |
| Valentinus at Pasau | 440 |
| Severinus, missionary in Noricum, d. | 482 |
| Kilian at Wurzburg | 643 |
| Boniface in Saxony and Hessia | 719 |
| Boniface in Bavaria | 739 |
| Sturmi founds monastery at Fulda | 744 |
| Charlemagne's wars with Saxons | 772–804 |
| Bp. Arno in Hungary | 796 |

| | |
|---|---|
| Archbp. Ebo at Holstein | 823 |
| Anskar in Denmark | 826 |
| Anskar visits Sweden | 829, 853 |
| Bp. Gautbert in Sweden | 835 |
| Ardgar in Sweden | 851 |

| | |
|---|---|
| Baptism of Bogoris king of Bulgaria | 863 |
| Methodius and Cyril in Moravia | 863 |
| Baptism of Bohemian Duke Borzivoi | 871 |
| Boso, Apostle of the Wends | 936 |

| | |
|---|---|
| Hakon, first Christian king of Norway | 936–44 |

| | |
|---|---|
| K. Wenceslav in Bohemia | 938 |
| Hungary, first Magyar Christians in | 949 |
| Queen Olga of Kiev visits Constantinople | 955 |

| | |
|---|---|
| Baptism of Danish king Harald and his army | 972 |
| Earl Hakon re-establishes paganism in Norway | 977 |

| | |
|---|---|
| Bohemia, Bp. Adalbert in | 982 |
| Vladimir, Baptism of | 988 |

| | |
|---|---|
| Sweyn re-establishes paganism in Denmark | 991 |
| Olof, first Christian king of Sweden | 993–1024 |
| Olaf Tryggvason, forcible conversion of Norway by | 1000 |

| | |
|---|---|
| King Stephen of Hungary | 997–1038 |
| Adalbert martyred in Prussia | 997 |

L

# HOW THE GOSPEL SPREAD

CONVERSION OF SCANDINAVIA AND EASTERN EUROPE
(*Continued*).

DENMARK AND SCANDINAVIA.

| | |
|---|---|
| Bp. Gotebald in Denmark | 1014 |
| Olaf Haraldson (of Norway) compels his northern subjects to be baptized | 1015–30 |
| Botvid, first native Swedish missionary | 1082 |

CENTRAL AND EASTERN EUROPE.

| | |
|---|---|
| Otto, missionary in Pomerania | 1124–39 |
| Vicelin, missionary to the Wends | 1125 |
| Vladimir II. | 1126 |
| General massacre of the Wends | 1157 |
| Esthonia, Forcible conversion of | 1219 |
| Prussia, Forcible conversion of | 1238–83 |
| Finland, Conversion of | 1240 |
| Lithuania, Conversion of | 1386 |
| Bp. Sergius in Russia, d. | 1392 |
| Stephen of Perm | 1401 |

In order to form some conception of the general progress of missionary work in Europe it may be worth while to note its development at two or three different epochs.

**Christianity in 312.**—Let us take for example the year 312 in which, after the battle of the Milvian Bridge, Christianity finally ceased to be a prohibited religion, and was sanctioned by the authority of Constantine.

At this time the total Christian population in the world was about four millions, of which somewhat less than half was to be found in Europe. Every Christian community of any size had its own bishop, and the number of bishoprics in Europe was then about 700. The only district of any size in which the Christians formed more than half the population was the southern part of Thrace to the north of the Sea of Marmora. The districts in which the Christians formed an important section of the population and exercised an influence upon the life of the whole community would include Rome and Southern Italy, and the coastal region of central Italy, also Spain, the south coast of France and the coastal districts of Thessaly and Macedonia. The districts in which small and scattered Christian communities were to be found included the greater part of the Balkan peninsula and parts of south-west Hungary and lower Austria, and the north-eastern portion of Italy, also southern Britain. Lastly, the districts in which but few traces of Christianity were to be found included north-west Italy, central and northern France, Holland and Belgium, Germany and the greater part of Austria and Hungary, also the north and north-west coasts of the Black Sea.

**Christianity in 600.**—Let us pass over another three centuries and consider what was the state of Europe from a missionary standpoint at the end of the sixth or the beginning of the seventh century. By the year 600 Christianity was firmly established throughout Ireland. In Scotland many centres of Christian influence had been established by Columba and his successors; the Britons in Wales and Cornwall were Christians and Christianity, which had been preached by Augustine in Kent, was beginning to spread amongst the Saxons. In the rest of England there may perhaps have been tiny Christian communities which had survived the devastating attacks of the Saxons.

At this time by far the greater part of France was Christian, though Columbanus and his fellow-missionaries, the centre of whose work was Luxeuil, in the Vosges mountains, found many who were ignorant of the Christian faith.

In Spain the Gothic king Reccared having recently renounced his Arian faith and declared himself a catholic, Christianity prevailed throughout the country, though the practice of idolatry was by no means extinct.

In Italy traces of paganism were to be found specially in the south. In the north the Lombards were still Arians. In the Balkan Peninsula the Christianity taught by Ulfilas had well-nigh disappeared. Christianity prevailed in Constantinople and throughout Greece, but the greater part of the northern half of the peninsula was still pagan. In Austria the inroads of the barbarians at the close of the fifth century had blotted out most of the Christian communities which had existed in Noricum and other parts of Austria, and few, if any, traces of the work accomplished by Severinus survived. Two and a half centuries were to elapse before missionary work was to be restarted.

In Germany the Christianity, which had been established at many different centres, especially in the western districts before the end of the fourth century, had been largely obliterated by the invasion of the Alemanni and other tribes, and a century was to elapse before the work of Boniface began.

In Holland, Denmark, Scandinavia, and Russia, as far as we know, no missionary work had as yet been attempted.

**Christianity in 900.**—Passing over another three centuries we come to the year 900. By this date missionary work had been attempted in Denmark by Archbishop Ebo, and by Anskar, but the country remained heathen. In Sweden missionary work had been started in Gothland, and in one or two other districts, but Sweden had still to wait nearly a century before it received its first Christian king. In Norway no missionary work had as yet been attempted. Holland, which had become nominally a Christian country, had recently suffered much from the invasion of the Northmen, who had destroyed a large number of churches, especially in the neighbourhood of Utrecht.

In Germany Charlemagne's thirty years' war with the Saxons had resulted in the forcible extension of the Christian church in their midst, and with the exception

## A GENERAL SURVEY

of Prussia, and Pomerania to which missionaries had not yet penetrated, and of Wendland in the north-east, where a few unsuccessful attempts had been made to evangelize its peoples, Christianity had spread throughout nearly the whole of what now constitutes Germany. In Austria Methodius had organized a Christian Church in Moravia; Hungary had been recently overrun by the heathen Magyars; in Bohemia Duke Borzivoi had been baptized, but his example had not been followed by that of his subjects. In other districts isolated Churches existed, but missionary work was at a standstill.

In Greece the last of the pagan inhabitants of the Peloponnesus had recently been forced to accept Christian baptism. Under the influence of Bogoris, king of Bulgaria, who was baptized in 863, a Bulgarian Church had been established and active missionary work was being carried on in Macedonia and other parts of the Balkan Peninsula.

**Christianity in 1000.**—A century later, that is in 1000, Christianity and paganism were still struggling for the supremacy in Denmark; and Norway and Sweden had each received their first Christian king. In Norway the second Christian king, Olaf Tryggvason, who came to the throne in 1000, was about to commence his campaign for the forcible destruction of heathenism.

In Prussia a first unsuccessful attempt to preach the Christian faith had resulted in the martyrdom of Adalbert. The rest of Germany, with the exception of Wendland and Pomerania, was nominally Christian. In Hungary King Stephen was earnestly promoting the conversion of his Magyar subjects. In Poland a bishopric had been established at Posen, and king Boleslav was endeavouring to secure the conversion of his Slav subjects.

In Russia the baptism of Vladimir (in 988) had been followed by many of his subjects and Christianity was beginning to extend, especially in the neighbourhood of Kiev.

## HOW THE GOSPEL SPREAD

The evangelization of European Russia occupied several centuries and even within recent years there were still many pagans to be found in the district of Kazan.

### MISSIONARIES IN EUROPE, 300-1200.

| Name. | Scene of labour. | Date. |
|---|---|---|
| Ulfilas | Bulgaria, d. | 381 |
| Martin, bp. of Tours | Central France | 316-97 |
| Patrick | Ireland | 432 |
| Ninian | Southern Picts, Scotland, d. | 432 |
| Valentinus | East Bavaria | 440 |
| Severinus | Noricum (S. Austria) | 482 |
| Eleutherius | Tournai, Flanders | 456-532 |
| Fridolin | Amongst Alemanni and in Black Forest | circ. 500 |
| Medardus | Tournai, Flanders, d. | 563 |
| Columba | Iona, W. Scotland, d. | 567 |
| Augustine | Kent | 597-604 |
| David | Wales | 601 ? |
| Kentigern (St. Mungo) | Strathclyde, d. | 603 |
| Columbanus | Gaul, Switzerland, N. Italy, d. | 610 |
| Paulinus | Northumbria | 625-633 |
| Eustasius | N. Bavaria, d. | 635 |
| Livinus | Brabant | 633 |
| Aidan | Lindisfarne, Northumbria | 635-51 |
| Trudpert (Irish hermit) | Black Forest | 600 ? |
| Kilian (Irish Bp.) | Black Forest | 626 |
| Gall | Switzerland, d. | 646 |
| Eligius | Frisia (Holland) | 641 |
| Cedd | Mercia | 653 |
| Wilfrid | Frisia | 678 |
| Wilfrid | Sussex | 681 |
| Willibrord | Frisia, Utrecht | 692-738 |
| Boniface | Germany | 680-755 |
| Sturmi | Bavaria | 744 |
| Gregory of Utrecht | Frisia and R. Ems district | 781 |
| Lebuin (Liafwin) | Frisia, d. | 775 |
| Willehad | Frisia, d. | 789 |
| Arao, Bp. of Salzburg | Hungary | 796 |
| Liudger | Frisia, d. | 809 |
| Ebo, Archbp. of Rheims | Jutland, Denmark | 823 |
| Anskar | Denmark and Sweden | 826-65 |
| Gautbert | Sweden | 835 |
| Ardgar | Sweden | 851 |
| Methodius and Cyril | Moravia | 863 |
| Adalbert | Prussia | 997 |
| Otto | Pomerania | 1124 |
| Vicelin | Wendland | 1125 |

## XVI

## RESULTS OF CHRISTIAN MISSIONS IN EUROPE

**WERE Christian Missions a failure?**—We can understand, and to a large extent sympathize with, the point of view of the man who, after studying all the information that is available relating to the spread of Christianity throughout Europe, should ask the question, Was the work accomplished by Christian missionaries after all a failure? Did they, or their successors, witness the accomplishment in any intelligible sense of the word, of the task which they attempted?

The question is one which is being asked by many members of the Christian Church to-day as well as by those who stand outside its ranks.

Disheartened by the failure of the Church to solve the social problems that have arisen in successive ages, and by the fact that it appears to be out of touch with the aspirations of " Labour " to-day, many are beginning to ask whether the conversion of Europe to a nominal acceptance of Christianity marked as great a step forward in the uplifting of the human race as has generally been supposed.

Before we can decide as to the success or failure of Christian Missions, whether past or present, we must ask ourselves what we conceive to have been, or to be, the purpose of these Missions.

**The purpose of Christian Missions.**—The teaching of Christ and the interpretation of His teaching by the writers of the New Testament lend no support to the theory that the preaching of the Gospel is one day to result in the conversion into saints of all the people on earth. Christ anticipated that those who would become His disciples would act as a light in the world, singly as individuals, and collectively as a Church, and that they would reflect a light upon the world which would cause men to recognize the presence and glory of God manifested in their midst.

The life which Jesus Christ lived on earth cannot be described as a failure on the ground that it failed to transform, or to raise to a higher level, the lives of any large proportion of His fellow-countrymen, nor can the lives which Christian missionaries have lived be regarded as having failed on the ground that the ideals by which their lives were inspired and which enabled them to produce some faint reflection of their Master's character, have not become dominant factors in the lives of nations or of individuals.

It must sorrowfully be admitted that the pages of European history are stained with a long series of crimes, which were committed in the name of religion, and that the official representatives of the Church have not always been the champions of truth and freedom. We must, however, remember that the success or failure of Christian Missions in any age is to be judged not so much by the outward results which can be registered and tabulated, but by the opportunities which they afford to the inhabitants of the various countries to see for themselves the embodiment of Christian ideals, to behold, in fact, a real though incomplete, reproduction of the life of Jesus Christ.

By the measure and degree in which such opportunities have been afforded must the success of missionary work in all lands and in all ages be judged.

Missionary work in the past has been a success in so far as it can be shown that the lives of the missionaries, and the lives of some of those whom they have influenced, have furnished to the age in which they lived an object lesson of the results which the acceptance of the Christian faith can produce. No missionary work has been a failure in any country if, as a result of the lives lived by the missionaries amongst its inhabitants one and another have been able to say, as Pompilia said concerning Caponsacchi:

> " Through such souls . . .
> God stooping, shows sufficient of His light
> For us i' the dark to rise by. And I rise."

**The reproduction of the Christian character.—** The goal of Christianity, and therefore the goal which the missionary has primarily in view, is the reproduction of the Christian character. The chief means whereby he may hope to attain his goal is the manifestation of the one only character which has adequately revealed to the world the nature of God. Other religions have claimed to reveal God by means of a series of doctrinal statements, but no other religion has offered to the world an ideal character and claimed that this character was itself a divine revelation. The Christian missionary, if he is to make this revelation effective, must be able not only to describe the character of Jesus Christ but to reflect it.

The first great missionary in a letter that he wrote to the Christians at Corinth, for whose conversion he had laboured, could speak of himself and of other Christians as " reflecting as a mirror the glory of the Lord."

**Missions and social problems.**—The appeal, however, which the missionary consciously, or unconsciously, addresses to individuals is not inconsistent with his recognition of an obligation to concern himself with the social problems that arise amongst the people to whom he ministers. If the early missionaries laid primary emphasis upon the appeal which they made to individuals, to repent and do deeds worthy of repentance, they none the less proved themselves to be philanthropists, reformers and educators. It was they who provided the initial impulse towards new and higher standards of national practice, truth and purity, and to their credit must be placed the gradual spread of religious and secular education throughout Europe. Moreover the fact that their ideals too often failed of realization must not blind our eyes to the efforts which they made in days that are now forgotten. The present condition of Russia has suggested to many the question, Is it possible to trace a connection between the methods pursued by the early missionaries in Russia and the wide-spread repudiation of Christianity by its inhabitants to-day? We must admit that the methods by which Christianity was spread throughout a large part of Russia were far from being ideal, but at the same time we must recognize that had not the careful and systematic education which Vladimir initiated, at the instigation of the Christian missionaries, been repudiated by its later rulers, who claimed control over the national Church, the condition and prospects of Russia would be far different from what they now are. It is, in fact, altogether unjust to hold the early missionaries responsible for results which followed the repudiation of their policy by those who came after them.

**The use of physical force.**—In this brief survey of the spread of Christianity throughout Europe we have had frequent occasion to allude to the large part which the employment of physical force played in the conversion of its peoples. From the time of St. Augustine onwards it became more and more generally recognized that it was right to use force in order to compel heretics to recant their errors, or pagans to abandon the practice of heathen customs. Protesting voices were raised from time to time, *e.g.* by Chrysostom Bishop of Constantinople, Hilary Bishop of Poitiers, Martin Bishop of Tours, Alcuin of York, and Raymond Lull, missionary to the Moslems. Thus Chrysostom wrote, " It is not lawful for Christians to overthrow error by force and violence, but they should labour for the conversion of men by persuasion, speech and gentleness." Hilary wrote, " God will not have a forced homage. Woe to the times when the divine faith stands in need of earthly power." Raymond Lull wrote with reference to the policy of the Crusaders, "They think they can conquer by force of arms: it seems to me that the victory can be won in no other way than as Thou, O Lord Christ, didst seek to win it by love and prayer and self-sacrifice." Despite however, these and the other protests which were made from time to time, the practice of employing force spread from land to land. In cases where the use of force facilitated the introduction of education and thereby rendered possible an intelligent appreciation of the teachings of Christianity, the harm resulting from its employment was less conspicuous, but the experience alike of ancient and modern Missions abundantly proves the truth of Raymond Lull's statement that victory over evil can be won in no other way than by love and prayer and self-sacrifice.

**Ancient and modern Missions.**—Another lesson which a careful study of early Missions in Europe serves to teach is the need of patience in the prosecution of missionary enterprises.

Critics of modern missions, and specially of Missions in India and the Far East, sometimes urge that the rate of progress is so small that centuries will be needed before any large proportion of the inhabitants of these countries become Christians. A comparison of the rate of progress of missionary work in Europe with that in India and the Far East is, however, full of encouragement to the modern missionary. It took more than a thousand years to secure the nominal conversion to Christianity of the northern half of Europe, but no one who has made a careful study of modern Missions anticipates that a similar space of time will elapse before Christianity has spread throughout the whole world. In so far as Government returns and the most trustworthy missionary reports supply data wherewith to form an opinion, it appears that the progress of Christian Missions in India during the last forty years has been five times as rapid as was the progress of Missions in Europe during the thousand years which followed the conversion of Constantine. If we accept the evidence of the last four returns of the Government Census, we should be justified in saying that, should the rate of increase of the Christian community relative to the whole population that has taken place during the last thirty years be maintained, in 160 years from now the whole of India will be Christian.*

Moreover, if we turn from India to China we find that the progress of Christian Missions in recent years has been much more rapid than has been the case in India. So far then is it from being the case that a comparison between the rate of progress of ancient and modern Missions affords grounds for discouragement the opposite is the case. When we compare the rate of progress in the principal mission fields of to-day with that in Europe in the past and remember that whatever progress has been attained during recent times has been attained without any appeal to physical force we cannot but face the future with hope and expectation. Apart, however, from any consideration of the comparative rates of Christian Missions in ancient and modern times, the question has been raised by the critics of modern Missions,

**Have Christian Missions benefited mankind?—** Is it quite certain that Europe has benefited sufficiently by the labours of Christian missionaries in the past to justify an attempt to promote Christian Missions elsewhere? Inasmuch as the whole progress of Western civilization is inextricably mixed up with the establishment of Christian Churches in Europe, it is not easy to say what reforms, or what social achievements, can be credited to the spread of the Christian faith. There are, however, at least three outstanding developments for which, it

---

\* See " History of Christian Missions," by the author, p. 119.

may be confidently claimed, that the teaching of Christianity was responsible.

These are—1. The increased value set upon child-life. 2. The care of the sick and afflicted. 3. The abolition of slavery.

1. Dr. Döllinger has stated that at the time when Jesus Christ was born the exposition of infants by parents, who desired the death of their children, was "the ordinary practice of the day" in Southern Europe. It was the protests of Tertullian and other Christians which first helped men to regard the practice as evil and to secure its abolition; and their action was a necessary outcome of their acceptance of the Christian faith. In the sixth century it became the general custom to place a marble vessel at the entrance of Christian churches for the reception of infants exposed by their parents.

Christianity is indeed the only faith which has ever inculcated a genuine sympathy for childhood. Jesus Christ was the only teacher of antiquity who cared for childhood as such, and who loved children for the sake, not of what they mght become, but of what they were. His statement, "of such is the kingdom of God," constituted a completely new revelation, and one which even His own followers were very slow to appreciate. The doctrine that all children are born heirs of perdition and subjects of the wrath of God, which was held by many Christians in early and mediæval times, tended to obscure the full significance of His teaching, but it may, nevertheless, be claimed that to the spread of Christian influence throughout Europe was directly due the increased value set upon child-life which has been one of the most striking developments that have taken place during the last two thousand years.

2. The second development for which it may be claimed that Christianity was responsible relates to the cause of the sick and afflicted. At the time of the Christian era the whole Roman empire did not contain

a single hospital. The first of which any record exists and which was the forerunner of those that are now to be found in almost every town in Christendom, was built at Rome by a Christian lady named Fabiola, in the fourth century. Another founded by the Christian emperor Valens at Cæsarea dates from about 375. The French equivalent for hospital Hôtel-Dieu, suggests its Christian origin. Medical Missions on the lines with which we are familiar to-day were unknown in the early centuries. Nevertheless it can be shown that the sick and afflicted and, in particular, the lepers, of whom Lazarus was regarded as the patron, were an object of special care to the Christian missionaries, and that it was as a result of their labours that the obligation, which rests alike upon individuals and communities to care for the sick and afflicted, came to be generally recognized.

3. Again and again in the record of early Christian Missions we read of the protests made by missionaries against the ill-treatment of slaves and of efforts made by them to secure their enfranchisement. We read, for example, of 250 slaves being baptized and set free by Ethelwalch, king of the South Saxons at the instigation of Wilfrid, of Pope Nicholas urging upon Bogoris king of Bulgaria, after he had received Christian baptism, the duty of setting free his slaves, and of the general amelioration in the condition of the large slave population of Russia which resulted from the teaching of the first missionaries. When at length the principles underlying the teaching of Christ came to be more perfectly understood, and slavery was recognized as wrong, its abolition was secured by men who were earnest Christians, and who were moved to take action by the conviction that its continuance was inconsistent with the acceptance of the Christian faith.

Whilst we are constrained to admit that the spread of Christianity throughout Europe and the Christian Church or Churches which were subsequently developed have failed to solve many social problems which cry aloud for attention, we believe that the benefits which Christianity has conferred upon Europe more than justify any efforts that can be made to-day to evangelize the non-Christian races of the world. In Europe, moreover, Christianity has by no means spoken its last word. Its influence in many of the councils of the nations was never stronger than it is at the present time, and the principles of truth and of justice to the weak which the victory of the allied powers has vindicated are principles which were first taught throughout Europe by Christian missionaries, though the final outcome of their teaching is not yet apparent. In a recent speech relating to the European war President Wilson said, "Christianity is the only force in the world that I have ever heard of that does actually transform life. And the proof of that transformation is to be found all over the Christian world."

As we turn from the story of the past to contemplate the outlook of Christian Missions in other lands we may confidently anticipate that the modern successors of the early missionaries, taught by the failures and mistakes of their predecessors, will be instrumental in securing the acceptance of Christian ideals of life and conduct in other lands to a far greater extent than the world has yet seen.

# INDEX

ADALBERT, bp. of Julin, 129
Adalbert, Bp., in Bohemia, 161
Adalbert, Archbishop of Prague, 134 f., 166
Adam of Bremen, 96
Adamnan, biographer of Columba, 61, 63 f.
Adda, missionary in Mercia, 81
Adrian, Pope, supports work of Methodius, 103
Agilbert, Bp., in Wessex, 80
Aidan missionary in Northumbria, 75–8, 166
Aix, Augustine at, 68 f.
Alani in Spain, 35 ; in Gaul, 46
Alaric king of the Goths, 19
Alban, St., Martyrdom of, 66 f., 160
Albert of Bremen in Livonia, 155 f.
Alcuin of York, 91 ; Letters of, 105
Aldhelm bp. of Sherborne, 80
Alemanni, 98 ; Columbanus preaches to the, 49 ; in Germany, 109
Amanaburg, Boniface founds monastery at, 110
Amandus in Holland, 88
Ambrose, re spread of Christianity in N. Italy, 28
Ancient and Modern Missions, 171 f.
Andrew, St., his connection with Russia, 7
Angles, in Mercia, 80 f.; in Scotland, 64 f.
Anna, wife of Vladimir, 150
Anskar, in Denmark, 93–6, 161, 166 ; in Sweden, 142, 144, 161
Apostolic Missionaries, 7
Aquitaine, Devastation of, 46
Ardgar in Sweden, 161, 166

Arles, Council of, 26, 42, 66, 160 ; Augustine consecrated at, 70
Arno bp. of Salzburg, 105, 161, 166
Asceticism of Columba, 48
Asia Minor, Early Missions in, 6 f.
Askold, Russian prince, 146
Asturis, Severinus at, 99
Athanaric king of the Goths, Persecution of Christians by, 16
Athens, Christian Church in, 14
Attalus emperor of Rome, 28
Attalus companion of Columbanus, 31
Augustine disapproves of destruction of heathen temples, 28 ; re fame of St. Vincent, 34
Augustine, of Canterbury, 68–72, 160, 166
Aurelius, Marcus, 12
Austria, Early missions in, 98–108
Autbert companion of Anskar, 94
Auxentius biographer of Ulfilas, 17 f.
Avoundus king of Sweden, 142 f.

BALKAN Peninsula, 7, 9 f., 14–23
Bamberg, Otto Bp. of, 129, 132
Basil, Emperor, sends missionaries to Slavonic tribes in Greece, 15
Batavi in Holland, 88
Bavaria, 98 ; Missions in, 113 f., 119
Bede, re the early British Christians, 67 ; re St. Augustine, 70 ff.
Benedict, Revival of monasticism by, 10 ; at Monte Cassino, 30
Benedict companion of Archbishop Adalbert, 134
Bernard, missionary in Friesland, 91
Bernard, Spanish missionary in Pomerania, 124 f.

M

# INDEX

Bernicia, Kingdom of, 77
Bernwin in Isle of Wight, 80
Beroea, Christian Community at, 14
Bertha, Queen, 70
Berthold missionary to Lieflanders, 155
Betti, missionary in Mercia, 81
Bible, Gothic, translated by Ulfilas, 16 f.; Greek and Latin translations of, 27; Translation of, into Slavonic, 102
Binna companion of Boniface, 111
Biorn king of Sweden, 142
Birinus missionary in Wessex, 79 f.
Birka, Attack on by Avoundus, 142 f.
Blandina, martyr at Lyons, 40
Bobbio, Monastery of, 31
Bogoris, Bulgarian prince, 20–3; 161, 165
Bohemia, Conversion of, 104
Boleslav III. conquers Pomerania, 123 f.
Boniface, Life and work of, 109–19, 161, 166
Boniface, Pope, Letter of Columbanus to, 50
Boris, see Bogoris
Borzivoi, Bohemian chief, 104, 161, 165
Boso Apostle of the Wends, 122, 161
Botvid, Swedish missionary, 162
Bregenz, Columbanus at, 49
Bridget, St., 58
Bruno missionary in Prussia, 135
Bruto a Saxon chief, 121
Bulgaria, Goths in, 15; Later missions in, 19–23
Bulosudes Magyar prince, 106

CANDIDA CASA, Monastery of, 85
Canterbury, Augustine at, 70
Canute, Missionary work in Denmark, supported by, 97
Callistus bishop of Rome, 25
Cammin in Pomerania, 126
Carelians, Missions to the, 155
Carloman assists Boniface, 114
Catacombs in Rome, 27 f.
Ceadwalla, King, 80
Cedd, Bishop, 77, 81 f., 160, 166
Celtic language in South of France, 41

Celtic missionaries, Standard of learning of, 51
Cenchrea, Christian Church in, 14
Chad, Bp., 77, 82
Charlemagne, 90 f., 161; Wars of, against the Saxons, 119; Letters of Alcuin to, 105
Chichester, See of, 84
Child-life, Value of, as taught by Christian missionaries, 173
Christian, Bishop, in Prussia, 135 f.
Christian Missions, Purpose of, 167 f.
Clement of Rome, re state of the Church in Corinth, 14; re deaths of St. Peter and St. Paul, 25; re visit of St. Paul to Spain, 32
Clovis, Baptism of, 46 f., 160
Colman, Bp. of Lindisfarne, 78
Columba, St., 60–4, 160, 166
Columbanus, 160, 166; in France, 47–9; in Switzerland, 49 f.; in Italy, 31
Comagenis, Severinus at, 100
Constantine, Influence exerted by, 12 f.
Constantinople, Heathen in, 15
Constantius, Edict of, prohibiting heathen sacrifices, 28
Corbie, Monastery at, 93
Cordova, Martyrs at, 36
Corinth, St. Peter and St. Paul at, 7; Christian Church in, 14
Corman, missionary in Northumbria, 75
Cornelius, bishop of Rome, 27
Cornwall, Conversion of, 85, 163
Crimea, Goths in, 15
Cross, The wearing of the, by converts, 22 f.
Cuthbert, Letter of Boniface to, 118
Cynegils king of Wessex, 80
Cypharas, Constantine, in Bulgaria, 20
Cyprian, his relations to Spanish Church, 33
Cyril missionary in Moravia, 102 f.

DACIA, Ulfilas in, 15
Dalmatia, Christian communities in, 14
Danes, in Ireland, 58; in Scotland, 64; in Esthonia, 156

# INDEX

David, St., of Wales, 85, 160, 166
Daniel, bp. of Winchester, 80, 111 f.
Dead, Prayers on behalf of heathen, 23, 89
Deception, Use of pious, by missionaries, 22
Deira, Kingdom of, 77
Demmin, Bp. Otto at, 129 f.
Denmark, Early Missions in, 93
Deventer, Lebuin at, 90; Liudger at, 91
Diocletian, Persecution by, 33
Dionysius the Areopagite reputed to have visited Gaul, 40
Dir, Russian prince, 146
Diuma, missionary in Mercia, 81
Dnieper, Baptisms in R., 150
Dokkum, Willehad at, 91; Boniface at, 117
Domnus a Pannonian bishop, 98
Dorchester, Birinus Bp. of, 80
Drontheim, Assembly at, 138 f.

Eadbald, king of Kent, 72
East Anglians, Conversion of, 72–4
East Saxons, Conversion of, 72, 82 f.
Eata, bp. of Lindisfarne, 77
Ebba, Queen, in Wessex, 84
Ebo, Archbishop of Rheims, 93, 161, 166
Edwin king of Northumbria, 74
Egbert, Archbp., Letter of Boniface to, 118
Eleutherius bp. of Tournai, 160, 166
Elfleda daughter of King Oswy, 81
Eligius, missionary to the Frisians, 160, 166
Elvira, Council of, 34 f., 160
England, Conversion of, 66–87
Eoban, Bp. of Utrecht, 116
Eorpwald king of East Anglians, 73
Epirus, 14, 19
Eric king of Jutland, 94
Eric king of Norway, 139
Erik, Swedish king in Finland, 157
Esthonia, Conversion of, 156, 162
Ethelbert, King, 70 ff.
Eulalia a Spanish martyr, 34
Eusebius *re* methods by which Christianity was spread, 8 f.; *re* number of Christians in Rome, 25

Eustatius missionary in N. Bavaria, 166

Fabiola founds hospital at Rome, 174
Favianae, Severinus at, 100
Felix missionary in East Anglia, 73
Ferrer, Vincent, preaches to Jews in Spain, 38 f.
Finan, Bp. in Mercia, 81 f.
Finland, Missions in, 157, 162
Finnian of Movilla, 60
Finnish tribes in N. Russia, 153, 155
Formosus, Bp., in Bulgaria, 21
France, Early Missions in, 40–52
Franconia, Early Missions in, 109
Fridolin, missionary in Black Forest, 166
Frisia, Boniface in, 110, 116; Wilfrid in, 88, 160; Willibrord in, 88, 160
Frisians in Holland, 88
Fulda, Monastery at, 121
Fuldrad, Letter of Boniface to, 115
Fursey missionary in East Anglia, 73

GALATIA, Missions in, 6
Gall, St., at Bregenz, 49 f., 166
Gatianus, bp. of Tours, 42
Gaudentius companion of Archp. Adalbert, 134
Gautbert missionary in Sweden, 142, 161, 166
Gedania, Adalbert at, 134
Germanus bp. of Auxerre, 160; in Britain, 67; in Wales, 85
Germanus bp. at Kazan, 157
Germany, Missions in, 109–36
Gondophares Parthian chief, 7
Gorm king of Denmark, 97
Gotebald, bp., in Denmark, 162
Gothland, 164; West, 144
Goths, Conversion of the, 15–19
Gottschalk a Slavonic chief in Wendland, 122
Greece, Christian missionaries in, 14
Greek-speaking Christians in Italy, 26
Gregory bishop of Tours, 42
Gregory of Utrecht, 90, 166
Gregory, Pope, 68 f.
Gregory II., Pope, Letter of, to Boniface, 110

## INDEX

Gregory III., Pope, Letter from, to Boniface, 113
Gregory a missionary in Russia, 146
Groningen, Willehad at, 91
Gutzkow, Bp. Otto at, 130
Gylas the ruler of Transylvania, 106
Gytha wife of Vladimir II., 152

Hadebald, Bp., assists Anskar, 94
Hakon, king of Norway, 137 f., 161
Hakon, Earl, in Norway, 138, 161
Hamburg, Anskar at, 94
Harald Klak king of Denmark, 93, 97, 161
Harald Haarfagar first king of Norway, 137
Hardships endured by early missionaries, 52
Healing of the sick by missionaries, 9, 173 f.
Heathfield, Battle of, 74
Heavenfield, Battle of, 75
Hegesippus *re* state of the Church in Corinth, 14 f.
Henrick, Bp. of Upsala, 157
Herigar, Swedish chief, 142 f.
Heroism, Deeds of, performed by missionaries, 5
Hesse-Cassel, Boniface in, 110
Hessia, Boniface in, 110 f.
Hiddila missionary in I. of Wight, 80
Hilary bp. of Poitiers, 160
Holland, Early Missions in, 88-92
Holm, Sigfrid at, 156
Holstein, Ebo establishes a Mission at, 93
Honorius, Decree of, concerning heathen temples, 28
Horick king of Denmark, 95
Hosius bp. of Cordova, 35
Hospitals started by missionaries, 173 f.
Hungary, 98, 104; Early Missions in, 104-8
Huns in Gaul, 46
Ideals, Missionary, 168 f.
Igor Russian prince, 146
Illyria, Christian communities in, 14
Ilminsky missionary to the Tartars, 158

India, Missions in, compared with Missions in Europe, 172
Inge king of Sweden, 145
Innocent III. promotes conversion of Livonia, 155
Intercessory prayer, *see* Prayer
Iona, Monks of, 60 f.
Ireland, Early missions in, 53-8
Irenaeus, bp. of Lyons, 40 f.
Irish missionaries on the Continent, 53
Italy, Early Missions in, 24-31

Jaruman, Bp., in London, 83, 160
James, St., the patron saint of Spain, 7, 32
Jengis, Massacres by, 154
Jerome *re* decline of paganism in Rome, 28
Jews in Spain, 38 f.
John, St., Reference to missionary work in 3rd Epistle of, 8
John bishop of Mecklenburg, 122
John VIII., Pope, and the Bulgarians, 23
John VII., Pope, permits use of Slavonic liturgy, 103
Joseph of Arimathea, reputed to have visited England, 8
Julian, Attempts by, to purify heathenism, 30
Julin in Pomerania, 124, 126-8, 132
Juri, St., missionary to Tartars, 157
Justin Martyr *re* influence exerted by the lives and deaths of Christians, 8
Justinian, Emperor, orders the compulsory baptism of the Athenians, 15
Justus, bp. of Rochester, 71

Kalka, Battle of, 154
Kazan, St. Juri bp. of, 157 f.
Kentigern (Mungo), 59 f., 166
Kenwalch king of Wessex, 80
Kherson, Attack on, by Vladimir, 149 f.
Khozars in Crimea, 148
Kiev, 146 f., 150 f., 154
Kilian Irish missionary at Wurzburg, 109, 161, 166

# INDEX

Krive-Kriveyto Lithuanian pagan priest, 157
Kubansky, Lake, Monastery on, 154

LADOGA, Lake, Monastery on, 155
Laplanders, Missions to, 154
Lazarus reputed to have preached in Gaul, 8, 40
Lebuin, 90, 119–21, 166; at Marklum, 119 f.
Leon-Astorga site of bishopric in Spain, 33
Leprosum, Heathen temple at, 43
Lieflanders, Conversion of the, 155 f.
Lightfoot, Bp., *re* character of Aidan, 78
Lindisfarne, Island of, 76 f.
Lithuania, Conversion of, 156 f., 162
Liudger in Friesland, 91, 160, 166
Liudhard, Bp., at Canterbury, 70
Livinus, Irish Archbishop in Belgium, 160, 166
Livonia, Missions in, 155 f.
Lombards, 164
Louis the Pious, 93 f.
Lupus of Troyes in Britain, 67
Luxeuil, Columbanus at, 47 f., 163
Lyons, Persecution at, 40, 160

MACEDONIA, Early missions in, 6, 14 ; Bulgarians in, 19
Maestricht, Amandus bp. of, 88
Magyars in Hungary, 105 f.
Mark, St., in Alexandria, 7
Marmoutier, Monastery of, 43
Martel, Charles, Boniface protected by, 111
Martin of Tours, 42–6, 160, 166
Mary Magdalene reputed to have visited Gaul, 40
Maserfield, Battle of, 77
Maximin a Gothic bp. in North Africa, 19
Medardus at Tournai, 166
Medical Missions, 9, 173 f.
Meinhard Russian monk, 155
Mellitus bp. of London, 71 f., 82
Mendowg ruler of Lithuania, 156
Menevia (St. Davids), 85
Mercia, Conversion of, 80–2
Merida site of bishopric in Spain, 33

Methodius in Bulgaria, 20
Methodius and Cyril in Moravia, 102–4, 161, 166
Michael Greek Emperor, 20, 102
Milan, Edict of, 42
Mill, J. S., *re* influence exerted by Constantine, 12 f.
Milvian Bridge, Battle of, 162
Missionaries, The task essayed by, 6
Moesia, Goths in, 15
Monasteries in Spain, 34 f.; in Wales, 86 ; in Norway, 142 ; in Russia, 152 f.
Monasticism, Introduction of, into France, 10
Mongols, Invasion of Hungary by the, 107 f.; invasion of Russia, 153 f.
Monks as missionaries, 10 f.
Montanists in Rome, 27
Monte Cassino, Benedict at, 30 f.
Moors, The, in Spain, 36–9, 160
Moravia, Missions in, 101–4
Moslems, Missions to, in Spain, 37 ; in Russia, 158
Mozarabs in Spain, 36
Muller, Max, *re* translation of the Bible by Ulfilas, 17
Mungo, *see* Kentigern
Munich, Early Christian Community at, 109
Munster, Liudger at, 91

NAPLES, Pagan survivals in, 30
Nicholas I., Pope, Letter of, to Bogoris, 21 f.
Nicopolis, Christian community at, 14
Nidaros, King Olaf at, 139
Ninian, St., 59, 85, 160, 166
Nobili, Robert di, Use of pious deception by, 22
Noricum, Province of, 98
Northumbria, Conversion of, 74–9
Norway, Conversion of, 137–42
Novgorod, Christian school at, 151

ODO, Danish archbp. of Canterbury, 97
Olaf Haraldson of Norway, 140, 162

Olaf Tryggvason, King of Norway, 138 f., 161
Olaf king of Sweden, 143, 161
Olga, Baptism of, 146, 161
Olgerd, ruler of Lithuania, 156
Olof, the Lap-king first Christian king of Sweden, 144
Onega, Lake, Monastery on, 154
" Order of the Sword " in Livonia, 156
Origen in Athens, 14 ; *re* Christians in Britain, 66
Oswald king of Northumbria, 75 f.
Oswy, king of Northumbria, 81 f.
Otto, Bp., 162, 166 ; Missionary work of, 124–33

PAGAN observances, Attitude of missionaries towards, 28–30, 34, 44, 112, 114, 130, 136
Paganism, Survivals of, in Rome, 28 f. ; Attempts to revive, 29 f. ; in S. Italy, 30 f.
Palestine, Churches in, 6 f.
Palladius in Ireland, 54
Pannonia, 98
Passau, Pilgrim Bp. of, 106
Patrick, St., 54–8, 160 ; in Gaul, 46
Paul, St., Missionary labours of, 7, 32
Paul, Bp., in Bulgaria, 21
Paulinus,160; in Northumbria, 74,166
Paulitzky defends Bp. Otto, 126
Peada, king of the Middle Angles, 81 f.
Pelagius, teaching of, 67
Penda, King, 65, 74, 81 f.
Pepin, Willibrord helped by, 88
Percunos god of thunder, 133
Perm in S.E. Russia, 155
Perun, Russian idol, 147, 150
Peter, St., Missionary labours of, 7, 24 f.
Peter de Duisberg, author of the Prussian Chronicle, 133 f.
Philip II. of Spain, 38
Philippi, Christian community at, 14
Photius Patriarch of Constantinople, 21, 23
Physical force, Use of in the cause of Missions, 11–13, 22, 37, 65, 139 f. ; 170 f. ; Use of by missionaries, 132 f.

Pilgrim, Bp., in Hungary, 106
Picts, Conversion of the, 64 ; as missionaries in South Wales, 85
Picullos god of the lower regions, 133
Polycarp, 41 ; Letter of, to Christians at Philippi, 14 ; at Rome, 26 f.
Pomerania, Efforts to convert,123–33
Poole, Lane, *re* massacre of Moors in Spain, 38
Portugal conquered by the Alani, 35
Posen, Bishopric at, 165
Pothimus bishop of Lyons, 40
Potrimpos god of corn, 133
Prayers, Intercessory, of Martin, 441 ; of Columba, 61 ; Appeal by Boniface for intercessory, 112, 118 f.
Prosper of Aquitaine, 46
Prudentius a Spanish bishop, 33 f.
Prussia, Attempts to convert, 133–6, 162 ; Pagan customs of, 133 f.
Pyritz in Pomerania, 125 f.

RADBOD of Friesland, 89 f.
Ratisbon, Early Christian community at, 109
Reccared, Gothic King, 163 ; in Spain, 19 ; renounces Arianism, 36
Redwald king of East Anglians, 72 f.
Remigius, Bishop, 47
Results, Social, of Christian Missions, 172 ff.
Riga, Foundation of, 155
Rimbert biographer of Anskar, 95
Roderick king of Strathclyde, 60
Rome, St. Peter and St. Paul in, 7 ; Early Christian community in, 24 f., 27
Rostislav king of Moravia, 101 f.
Rostoff, Christian school at, 151
Roumania, *see* Dacia
Rupert bishop of Worms, 119
Rurik, Russian prince, 146
Russia, Conversion of, 146–58

SABA, St., his death as a martyr, 16
Sabert king of East Saxons, 72
Samland, Archbp. Adalbert in, 134 f.
Saturninus, bishop of Toulouse, 41
Saxons in Eastern Frisia, 92
Saxony (Wendland), Missions in, 121–3

# INDEX

Scandinavians in Scotland, 65
Schleswig, Mission school at, 94 f.
Scotland, Early Missions in, 59–65
"Scots," Use of the word, 59
Sebbi king of East Saxons, 83
Selenas, a bishop amongst the Goths, 18 f.
Selsey, Bishops of, 84
Serbia, Goths in, 15
Sergius, Russian missionary, 154, 162
Severinus, missionary in Noricum, 99, 161, 166
Sigebert king of East Anglians, 73
Sigebert king of East Saxons, 82, 160
Sigesarius, a Gothic bp. in Italy, 19
Sigfrid, Bp., in Sweden, 144
Sigfrid, Russian monk, 156
Siggo, murderer of Adalbert, 135
Sighere, king of East Saxons, 83
Sigibert of Austrasia, 47
Sigurd, Baptism of, 65
Simeon, a Bulgarian prince, 23
Simon Magus in Rome, 25
Skara, Thurgot missionary at, 144
Skene *re* work accomplished by monastic missionaries, 10 f.
Slave boys in Rome, 68
Slavery discouraged by Christian missionaries, 141, 174
Slaves, Missionary work accomplished by, 9
Slavonic Bible and Liturgy, 102–4
Social problems, failure of missionaries to solve, 167, 169 f.
Soldiers, Christian converts amongst, 26
Solovetsky monastery, 155
Sozomen *re* influence exerted by the lives of Christians in the Balkan Peninsula, 9
Spain, Early Missions in, 32–9
Stenkil king of Sweden, 145
Stephen, King, of Hungary, 106, 161
Stephen, missionary to the Ziranes, 155, 162
Stettin capital of Pomerania, 123, 127–32
Strathclyde, Kentigern bishop of, 60
Sturleson, Snorro, Norwegian historian, 137 f.
Sturmi, founds monastery at Fulda, 121, 161, 166
Suevi, in Spain, 35; in Gaul, 46, 55; near Lake Zurich, 49
Sussex, *see* Wessex
Sweden, Conversion of, 142–5
Sweyn king of Denmark, 97, 161
"Sword," "Order of the," 136
Syria, Churches in, 6

TACITUS *re* persecution of Christians in Rome, 24
Tartars, in Russia, 154; Missions to, 157
Temples, Destruction of heathen, 28, 43 f.
Tertullian *re* results of persecutions of Christians, 8; *re* Christians in Britain, 66
Teutonic Knights, Order of, 135 f.
Theodoric king of the Burgundians, 49
Theonus Bishop of London, 68
Thessalonica, Christian community at, 14
Thomas, St., Missionary labours of, 7
Thomas, bishop of Edessa, 7
Thor, Worship of, at Armagh, 58; in Norway, 138
Thurgot, missionary in Sweden, 144
Thuringia, Boniface in, 110
Toledo, Third council of, 36
Toulouse, Saturninus bp. of, 41
Tours, Battle of, 36
Transylvania, 105
Triglav a Slavic god, 128
Troitskaia monastery, 154
Trophimus reputed to have visited Gaul, 40
Trudpert, Irish hermit in Germany, 109, 166
Tryggvason, Olaf, 138 f.; in S. Ronaldsa, 65
Turholt, Monastery at, 94

UBSOLA, Destruction of idol temple at, 144
Ukskull, Meinhard at, 155
Ulfilas, Life and work of, 15–19, 161, 166
Unofficial missionaries, Work accomplished by, 8–10, 87

## INDEX

Upper classes, Conversion of, 13
Usedom, Bp. Otto at, 129 f.
Usbek, Khan, 154
Utrecht, Willibrord bishop of, 88 f.; Gregory of, 90; Boniface at, 110

VALDEMAR II. Danish King, 156
Valentinus at Passau, 161, 166
Valerian, Rescript of, 25; Persecutions by, 33
Vandals in Spain, 35; in Gaul, 46
Vicelin missionary to the Wends, 123; 162, 166
Victor Bishop of Rome, 26
Vienne, Persecution at, 160
Viken, Conversion of inhabitants of, 139
Vincent, St., of Zaragoza, 34
Vladimir, Conversion of, 146–51, 161
Vladimir II., 151 f., 162

WALES, Augustine interviews Bishops from, 71; Conversion of, 85
Wallachia, 107
Wenceslas king of Bohemia, 104, 161
Wendland, *see* Saxony
Wessex, Conversion of, 79 f., 83 f.
Westcott, Bp., *re* character of Columba, 62

Whitby, Conference of, 78, 160
Wight, Isle of, Conversion of, 80
Wilfrid, Bp., in Wessex, 84, 160; in Friesland, 88, 166
Willehad missionary in Friesland, 91 f., 166
Willibrord in Friesland, 88 f., 166
Wilson, President, on the outcome of missionary teaching, 175
Winchester, Bp. Wini at, 80
Wini, Bp., in Wessex, 80
Wittekind, Invasion of Friesland by, 91 f.
Wolgast, Bp. Otto at, 130
Wollin, Island of, 124, 126
Wratislav, Duke, in Pomerania, 126, 129 f.
Wulfram Archbp. of Sens, 89
Wulfhere son of Peada, 82 f.
Wurzburg, Kilian missionary at, 109

YADVIGA Polish queen, 156
Yagello ruler of Lithuania, 156 f.
Yaroslav, Russian prince, 151

ZACHARIAS, Pope, Letter of Boniface to, 115
Ziranes, Missions to the, 155
Zurich, Lake, Columbanus at, 49


THE END

www.ingramcontent.com/pod-product-compliance
Lightning Source LLC
Chambersburg PA
CBHW051741230426
43670CB00012B/2107